Praise for *Ramp*

"This is the book I wish I'd had twenty years ago"

— **JOHN FORAKER**, CEO of Once Upon a Farm and former CEO of Annie's

"This book provides an excellent framework to build a consumer brand in the 2020s."

— **MICHAEL MAUZE**, general partner of VMG Partners

" I wish I'd read this book before coaching teams that launched CPG startups!"

— **TOM EISENMANN**, Howard Stevenson Professor of Business Administration, Harvard Business School

"Every entrepreneur needs to read this book before launch. And each year thereafter!

— **ANDY WHITMAN**, managing partner of Loft Growth Partners

"The industry insights alone make this book worth its weight in gold. But far more valuable is how James Richardson forces you to stop, think, and be intentional about your growth."

— **JOHN SORIAL**, founder and managing partner of Tadah! Foods and 2019 *Shark Tank* winner

"*Ramping Your Brand* needed to be written, and it needs to be read. James offers a constructive and contrarian view that every CPG entrepreneur should consider. As investors, we spend a lot of time encouraging our partner brands to go narrow and deep, but the avalanche of available equity capital, open hands of retailers, and lure of easy early wins is proving harder and harder to resist. The patience and diligence urged by this book will serve you well and could save you millions of dollars wasted on marketing in advance of distribution and distribution in advance of proven, replicable success."

— **ROBERT BROWN**, co-founder and managing director of Encore Consumer Capital

"There hasn't been one book yet that can be a Founder's Bible ... until now. Read it and carry it around with you wherever you go. You will find yourself referencing it quite often."

— **GREG FLEISHMAN**, co-founder of Foodstirs and Purely Righteous Brands, former vice president of marketing of Kashi/Kellogg

"James is a keen observer of the consumer, and his insightful recap from the lessons of the 'unicorn' brands in CPG over the past decade is a great read. As an investor and an operator in CPG for the past 25 years, I haven't read any other book that so clearly captures these valuable lessons and factually challenges the ways that CPG brands were built decades ago. James' writing is entertaining, yet sharp, and will have you hooked whether you're an entrepreneur, investor, or operator."

— **APU MODY**, angel investor, former CEO of Lenny & Larry's, and president of Mars Food Americas

"For the new food entrepreneur, *Ramping Your Brand* is an essential road map to profitable and sustained growth. This entertaining book is written with nuggets of pragmatic wisdom, humor, and referenceable insights. Highly recommended."

— **DAVID DONNAN**, partner emeritus of A.T. Kearney

"Wow! *Ramping Your Brand* is a thoughtful, insightful, and detailed review of what it takes to become a meaningful and lasting brand in today's challenging landscape of consumer packaged goods. James' decades of experience within the CPG industry shines brightly, and the readers of *Ramping Your Brand* are provided valuable, specific, and relevant perspective and advice on how to build and then scale their brands. This is a must-read for anyone and everyone involved in creating, building, operating, or investing in CPG brands and businesses, if only to provide relevant context or to challenge your current thinking."

— **RODNEY J. CLARK**, managing partner of Aspect Consumer Partners

"Ramping Your Brand is loaded with actionable advice on how to effectively and sustainably achieve fast growth in CPG. A no-nonsense guide backed with research, behavioral science and James' one of a kind sense of humor make this a must read for early stage entrepreneurs ready to drop in and ride the ramp!"

— **TONYA DONATI**, co-founder of Mother Kombucha

"James blends a deep understanding of human behavior with empirical data about what has actually worked for early-stage brands. I laughed often and learned a lot. ... wish I could say that for other business books."

— **DAVID DeSOUZA**, President of HerbCo - Monterey Bay Spice

"*Ramping Your Brand* speaks right to the heart of the truth we need to hear as natural product entrepreneurs. James Richardson has an uncanny ability to get at the core issues and to communicate them thoughtfully and clearly. No BS, no fluff, just straight and honest sauce that is worth your time. I can't recommend this book enough, especially for anyone navigating the marketplace with an emerging brand."

— **TED ROBB**, CEO of New Barn Organics and partner of Stonewall Robb

"In this book, James Richardson crystallizes how to build a great brand and business in food/beverage, and he relies on lessons learned from intimate observation of both 'unicorns' and steady growth brands. His lessons are simple: focus on velocity; know more about your category than your retail buyer; keep everything simple; avoid unnecessary category expansion, etc. Read this before your next round of funding, and you may just make it your final raise."

— **TJ McINTYRE**, CEO of Bobo's Baked Goods

"This is a must-read for all emerging CPG brand leadership teams. James Richardson really gets you thinking correctly about what it takes to make a brand succeed."

— **VARANT MINASSIAN**, president of Maya Kaimal Foods

"*Ramping Your Brand* is, by far, the best CPG book out there. It gives entrepreneurs the foundational principles and tools they need to build the skate ramp of sustainable growth before they ride it. A must-read for anyone looking to reduce the risk and avoid the common pitfalls of launching and growing a CPG brand.

— **AUSTIN ARCHIBALD**, founder *of Rebel Creamery*

"*Ramping Your Brand* is packed with insights on the art and the science of incubating and scaling emerging CPG brands. James Richardson has synthesized and democratized over a decade of invaluable learnings into a one-of-kind, practical guide for entrepreneurs looking to ride the skate ramp.

— **WILL LISMAN**, Chief Commercial Officer at HumanCo, former General Manager at Amplify Snack Brands

RAMPING YOUR BRAND

RAMPING

HOW TO RIDE THE KILLER

YOUR

CPG GROWTH CURVE

BRAND

JAMES F. RICHARDSON, PhD

ISBN: 978-1-7334446-0-6 (paperback); 978-1-7334446-3-7 (hardcover); 978-1-7334446-1-3 (ebook)

Library of Congress Catalog Number: 2019911993
Printed in the United States of America
First Printing: 2019
23 22 21 20 19   5 4 3 2 1

Designed by Mayfly Design

PGS Press
Seattle, WA
james@premiumgrowthsolutions.com

To order, call PGS Press at 206–909–6129

CONTENTS

PART ONE: DESIGNING TO COMMAND A PREMIUM

PART TWO: MANAGING A SMALL EXPERIMENT

PART THREE: FINE-TUNING THE CONVERSION PLAYBOOK

PART FOUR: ACCELERATING TO SCALE

PREFACE

My first job in high school was a bizarre summer gig selling over-priced premium ice cream by the scoop, from a stand-alone kiosk inside a Burger King parking lot in Manchester, New Hampshire. It was 1988. Although Ben and Jerry's had retail shops all over New England by then, no one could foresee the incredible scale that premium ice cream brands would generate in the 1990s. Fancy scoops were still a treat. A Burger King parking lot, therefore, was just about the dumbest possible location you could have picked to sell ice cream at premium prices. The result? It was painfully dull sitting there with a trickle of customers every night, listening to my colleagues drivel on and on about Aerosmith, Guns N' Roses, and their myriad boy problems.

At that time in my life, I had no idea I would end up becoming a specialist in how to grow premium CPG brands in the United States. My brain was focused on academia. I just wanted to be a Professor of Something. I was a geek. I was socially awkward to a degree that still makes me wonder how I survived high school at all. I was medically underweight. I said stuff on a regular basis for which I should have gotten the shit kicked out of me. That probably hasn't changed, now that I think about it.

I began my adult working career as a cultural anthropologist, specializing in South Asia. (Trust me, there's a tiny thread of continuity here. Just hang on.) Aside from almost getting killed three times by complete strangers, living for nearly three entire years in South India was a positive, life-changing experience. Sadly, very few Americans commit to that kind of foreign cultural immersion, and I'll never regret what it taught me. My focus in graduate school was on how caste-stigmatized individuals manage the threat of being "outed" in urban Indian public life. Caste is largely an invisible social identity. It is discovered through conversation, gossip, and observations about with whom you spend your time. The individuals in question were middle-class "untouchables" trying to blend in and not stick out. Easier said than done. I didn't go to India to study this topic. India shoved this topic in my face almost as aggressively as the day I was drugged with Quaaludes in a Madurai restaurant, brought back to my nearby apartment, robbed, and left to pass out. That was my second day in India. I'm not a quitter.

So, when I decided to drop out of the academic tenure track in 2002, I was admittedly lost and blamed myself for abandoning a career that was basically sucking the life out of me. I had spent 14 years obsessing about being a Professor of Something. My research was fascinating to everyone I met, but I simply no longer enjoyed the field I was in. It had become embroiled in post-modern rants and adolescent in-fighting. Not to mention that tenure track jobs were almost impossible to find. I was staring at a multi-year process of stringing together one-year visiting professorships in highly undesirable U.S. locations, hoping someone elsewhere would retire or die. And how exactly do you get married living like an academic hobo? For me, leaving academia was like a divorce in which the two parties literally never speak to one another again. After nine years, that's a really bad outcome.

It took a long time for me to realize that walking away from academia saved me from a fate much worse than I had imagined at the time.

Initially, my future looked bleak. What the hell do you do with a PhD in cultural anthropology, outside of academia? In Chicago? In 2002? My options were limited. I'd met far too many clinically depressed anthropologists working inside ad agencies, doing the epitome of loaded inquiry to please account planners, to pursue that career path. I realized the calmer waters of market research would be a better home for my brain. So, I strategically circulated my resume in that direction and was recruited by a fast-growing, boutique market-research firm, The Hartman Group, based out of Bellevue, Washington. They specialized in health and wellness trends affecting consumer packaged goods. They wanted anthropologists. Their real expertise, however, was uncovering how—and, more importantly, why—consumers shifted from mainstream to natural/organic food consumption. We're talking major pantry-level conversion.

My first client was Whole Foods Market. Upon hearing that, I had a flashback to my first job selling overpriced ice cream. *Holy Sh*t! Did I actually get a PhD just to wind up back where I'd started in 1988? Are you kidding me? Is my life really a Mel Brooks routine?* Well, wait a minute. The pay was a lot better than that stupid kiosk gig, and my wrist wasn't constantly sore from scooping artisan ice cream, which, let me tell you, is much more viscous than the fake stuff.

After several years immersing myself in the pantries of American consumers at varying stages of adopting premium CPG brands, I led the creation of The Hartman Group's first ever consulting practice. What began as a side experiment, morphed into advising some of the top food and beverage companies in the world on how to alter their portfolios by modernizing existing brands and by acquiring new trademarks with advantaged growth potential.

From 2011–2017, my team and I engaged in a series of projects in which we had the opportunity to dive deep into the best practices of some of the most successful premium food and beverage brands that have scaled since the Great Recession. These are essentially the Wave 2 disruptors. We studied the commonly, if not universally, shared strategic moves they made (intentionally or not). This gave me a working knowledge of how to optimize growth for early-stage premium CPG brands more broadly. The theme, as you might suspect, is that the brands who have pulled off exponential growth since 2008 have been laser focused on consumer-centric innovation and on ensuring that they listened and followed the consumer as they carefully grew. This couldn't be more different than BigCo's approach to launching line extensions, a process that still focuses on trying to predict interest in tepid innovations and then launching them to maximal scale instantly.

This early work and my ongoing work with new entrepreneurs have culminated in a set of principles and practices that enable the strategically optimal growth of CPG brands. I share those best practices in this book, the first of its kind, tailored to the unique realities of building new-to-the-world, premium-quality CPG brands.

I believe this information should not be the exclusive purview of elite venture capitalists and wealthy public firms. It should be available to everyone who has the passion, integrity, and endurance to compete honestly for the consumer's money.

I hope you find it valuable.

ACKNOWLEDGMENTS

t's no easy feat to acknowledge all the support that goes into a piece of writing that sums up almost two decades worth of professional work. But here I go.

First of all, I thank my loving wife, Michelle, for supporting my transition into consulting years ago, even though I went kicking and screaming into it at the time. We anthropologists can be a bit difficult at times. As a former consultant herself, she gave me the good kick in the ass from someone in the field that I needed from time to time. I also thank Michelle for letting me pull equity out of our home to fund the development of this book and the research that went into it. I might as well also thank the Greater Seattle real estate market, too, while I'm on this topic. We've been lucky.

I also want to thank Harvey Hartman, founder of The Hartman Group, for literally pushing me into a consulting role in 2007 and for believing in my potential to rise to the occasion. The world doesn't need another cranky anthropologist whose mind can be put to much better use. I think we can agree on that. I also thank Laurie Demeritt, CEO of The Hartman Group, for letting me release some of the company's intellectual capital in this book for a founder audience that she personally supports and can greatly benefit from it but could never afford to pay anyone to generate it.

This past summer, I had five Beta readers review an early, complete draft of the manuscript. They represented the book's three key stakeholder groups: early stage founders, investors and BigCO CPG veterans. I thank Apu Mody, Bob Burke, Andrea Spirov, Robert Brown

xviii ACKNOWLEDGMENTS

and Tonya Donati for taking the time to do this and for offering their candid input and support.

On the production side, I thank my editor, Colleen Sell, a tour de force behind several business best-sellers, including Stephen Key's *One Simple Idea*. I'm lucky to have intrigued her so much with my topic. I'd also like to thank the Answers on Demand staff at AC Nielsen, Inc. for providing a superb, large, multi-category data pull in short order for a 'mere' solopreneur. I also thank my book designer, Ryan Scheife, of Mayfly Design, who managed to zip through a paternity leave to keep this book on track. His eye for detail is scary. My thanks go, too, to Vic Donati, of Donati Studio in St. Petersburg, for putting together a killer website for this book that beautifully accompanies his re-do of my corporate site. I also have to thank Chris Mauzé of Redfox Analytics for creating dashboards from raw Nielsen data in record time this past summer.

Finally, I thank Dorie Clark, best-selling author of *Stand Out* and *Entrepreneurial You*, and members of her Recognized Experts community who shared generously from their far greater publishing experience.

INTRODUCTION

t was 1:00 on a sweltering July afternoon in Phoenix, Arizona. I was sitting with a four-person team, roughly five hours into a two-day strategic planning session. Lunch had settled nicely in our bellies. As the discussion moved forward, a random thought came to me: *So, that's why everyone down here sets their AC thermostats to 80 degrees. Not only does it save money, but that's still 30 degrees colder than outside! No wonder these folks started a soft drinks company.*

Yes, my mind had wandered, and not just because of the stifling room temperature and post-lunch brain fog. Mostly, I was dreading the most awkward point in the two-day session: setting the 2019 revenue goal. Of course, my client didn't think it was going to be awkward at all. The founders had already shared their goal with me. Over the last four years, they had built a local business up to about $800,000 in gross sales—mainly in foodservice channels, with only a small portion in less stable traditional retail. Now, they had flown me in from Seattle to help plan a national launch to get them to $6 million in 12 months.

My client's revenue target might sound reasonable to someone new to the beverage industry and to the entrepreneurial path within it. What my client didn't realize was that the growth model they'd chosen was based on a hedge-fund level of risk for a new consumer packaged goods (CPG) brand. In their case, the draft plan involved stacking up national accounts (which they hadn't even approached yet) while simultaneously raising $7 million in investment capital. It could work out, if they had about $10 million on hand. Since they had only one-twentieth of that amount, it could wind up being a terribly short-lived, soft drink Ponzi scheme.

My case study and client work suggest that the vast majority of these types of premature national brand expansions result in lost retail accounts and wasted launch fees by the following year. Some lose more ground than others. The founders then go through a retrenchment that is painful, embarrassing, and damaging to the company's reputation in a well-connected trade. In many cases, the business simply goes under, because even angel investors are unlikely to continue donating to a business that is going downhill. No one likes to fund a small business rescue. Not even your parents.

That's why I felt obligated to reset my Arizona soft-drink client's most fundamental goal. Because it was just not wise. It was also strategically unnecessary in order to grow at a reasonably fast rate. The breakneck pace the founders had proposed would risk throwing away four years of hard work that was just beginning to pay off.

So now, halfway through the first day of their national-growth planning session, I had to convince my clients to slash their 2019 revenue goal. . . . And hope they wouldn't chase me out of the room and refuse to pay my second invoice. "We paid you for a plan to six million, bucko!"

Here is how that conversation unfolded:

Me: "So, Amy, remind me again of your revenue goal for next year." I casually broached the topic with the company's founder, as if I hadn't been dwelling on it for five days straight.

Amy: "Well, we'd like to be at six million."

Me: "Can you tell me how you and the team came to that figure?" I posed this open-ended question hoping to get a story. I needed to understand what was behind the most critical assumption of their otherwise professional 35-page business plan.

Amy: Five seconds or so of awkward silence. "Well . . . it's really the numbers that came out of the business plan."

Me: "Right, I know. But is there some specific reason why you want to grow more than six-fold in one calendar year?" I used the word *want* to subtly prompt her to see the goal's optionality and to reassess the assumptions and what-ifs upon which the goal was based.

Amy: "We just want to make more money," she said, her voice thick with emotion, suggestive of many hours of internal debate that had not been fully resolved.

Me: Looking directly into her eyes, I said, "Amy, I think that's great. You all deserve it. You're out there every weekend busting your ass in the Arizona heat, doing sampling. But what is really driving the need to suddenly make that much more money next year?"

Amy: She glanced at her husband, a co-founder who had to freelance in his old field to help make ends meet, and let out a deep sigh. "We've been working so hard for four years. We want to bring home more income from the business."

Me: "So, you want to pay yourselves more?"

Amy: "Yes," she said, her eyes lighting up as if I had acknowledged some dirty company secret that they weren't supposed to discuss.

Me: "Like I said, you all deserve it. I've never seen people work so damn hard at this phase of the business. What if you grossed two million next year? Would you be able to pay yourselves more?"

Amy: She paused to do some mental math, based on her fresh business plan. "Yes, that would work."

Me: "Great! Let's set that as our goal for the rest of our time together. Just so you understand, I didn't pick two million because I looked at how much your salaries would go up. I picked it because, at your current trailing revenue, doubling your size is the absolute highest you want to set your sights. It puts you on the path of exponential growth—which, if you sustain it, will bring you the money needed to scale fast and to generate sustainable profits. Make sense?"

Amy: "Yes," she said. Then she sighed again, as if some invisible burden had just floated off her shoulders.

Me: "So, if you agree, the question before us now is, how do we double your business in 2019?"

Amy relaxed back into her chair, as though even she felt their original target wasn't realistic. Phew! With that sticking point settled, I felt more confident the rest of the session would go okay. And we moved into the gritty details of planning the actions and potential reactions that would enable them to grow to $2 million in trailing revenue in a strategically defensible manner.

Why do so many CPG entrepreneurs who want to grow fast get sucked into unrealistic forecasts and stretch targets that are counter-productive, not based on bottoms-up data, and often financially ruinous?

The cynical might say, *It's greed, James.* But that is simply unfair and rarely the case. When you actually spend time with CPG entrepreneurs, you quickly realize most of these folks work long, hard hours to build their businesses and for very little, if any, pay. If these people are greedy, they're the dumbest greedy people I've ever met. Trust me, the greedy don't last 12 months as entrepreneurs in CPG.

I believe that CPG entrepreneurs fall into this trap for the same reason Amy confessed in our session. They're exhausted. They are tired of the low pay, the long hours, and the pay-off seeming to recede into the distance with every passing year. Who wouldn't feel like that at some point in the process of producing a business out of thin air?

Nevertheless, one law of CPG businesses is true no matter what the products or who launches them: to be profitable, you need to scale—not necessarily to $100 million but certainly not to only $500,000. Accelerated growth tends to solve the most fundamental entrepreneurial problem: low profitability and lack of available cash on hand. Sure, rapid growth often causes short-term cash-flow problems. But since fast growth makes the brand more attractive to investors and the retail trade, it's a problem you want to have.

Many entrepreneurial CPG brands struggle for growth early on. This is largely due to the product design itself, which simply doesn't attract retailer interest. In that case, the founders struggle to convince retail buyers to take them on. In other cases, they follow the bad advice of certain advisors and chase growth by increasing store counts and distribution, without doing the hard work to create memorability with consumers. Regardless of the cause of underperformance, many early-stage CPG brands grow almost linearly, crawling up the growth-rate equivalent of an ADA ramp. Most never make it to anywhere near $100 million in retail sales.

The question founders should ask themselves isn't, *Should I grow fast?* It's, *How fast can I reasonably grow and sustain that growth?*

Optimal Growth Pace for New CPG Brands

Numerous existing books (and textbooks) describe the basic growth principles of the CPG sector. So, you might be wondering why I've written a book about optimizing growth specifically for *young* CPG brands. Quite simply, my Arizona client is far from being the only budding CPG brand to shoot for the moon.

Every year, I meet more smart and capable entrepreneurs who either set unrealistically fast growth rates or want to grow quickly but struggle to grow fast enough to gain leverage with the trade. Many have a distorted view of what their optimal growth pace should be. This is due, in part, to the lack of transparency around the actual growth rates of new CPG brands and to the media's excessive coverage of unicorns (e.g., Caulipower).

Another contributing factor is that some CPG founders are influenced by the nearly vertical growth that happens when large public firms launch new brands or product-line extensions. That is definitely not an optimal (or even possible) growth pace for entrepreneurial CPG brands. BigCo's approach to growth only sets irrational expectations for founders who futilely aim for that kind of trajectory. (Figure 1)

No entrepreneurial CPG brand has *ever* matched the year-one (Y1) pace to scale shown in Figure 1. Not Halo Top. Not Chobani.

Figure 1: BigCo CPG Growth Model

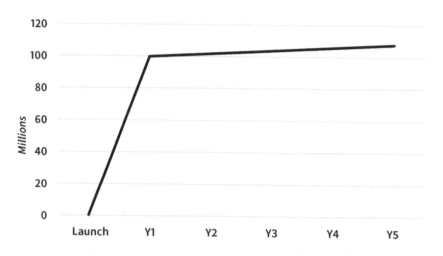

This graphic represents the ideal growth rate of a BigCo launch of a new brand or product-line extension. It is based on a composite of real-world cases from prior client work, not on actual sales data. Most successful launches have this shape, although few get this large.

Not Bai. Not Caulipower. Not CORE. No one. Nielsen calls these rare BigCo launches the *Sprinters*. For today's CPG entrepreneur, they are simply a mirage. Media-darling, early-stage, unicorn brands do grow slower than the BigCo launch model, but only slightly. These brands reach peak scale in two years instead of one. But that is still unrealistically fast for any founder to contemplate. Much too fast.

So, how can CPG entrepreneurs set a reasonably fast growth rate?

The fastest growth curve that CPG entrepreneurs can realistically plan to achieve looks like something no brand manager has seen before. This mystery curve is something I call the *Skate Ramp*. (Figure 2) The Skate Ramp is simply my name for the first half of the *Sigmoid curve*, or *S-curve*. This graphic representation of sales-volume growth over time is actually not new to business strategists. However, The

Hartman Group made waves when it re-awoke everyone's attention to it in a seminal 2013 industry white paper.[1]

Figure 2: The Skate Ramp

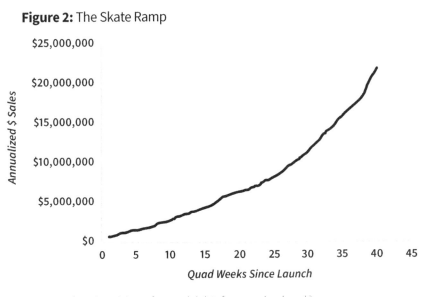

Four years of quad-week (every four weeks) data for a premium brand.[2]

The Skate Ramp is based on at least doubling sales every year—again and again and again. If you open a blank Excel worksheet and enter 250,000 in any cell and then double it repeatedly, moving to the right in a series, you will generate a line chart that looks awfully similar to a quarter-pipe ramp at your local skate park.

The logarithmic math behind the curve is exponential. Typically, however, the YoY growth rate decelerates as revenues approach $100 million (unless you're Kind, Chobani, or Skinnypop). The most important feature of this growth model is that the vast majority of growth is generated on the back half of the curve. In other words, founders are rewarded for their patience in scaling.

---

1. *Hartbeat Exec,* "Riding the Killer Curves of Growth," Volume 3, Issue 2, 2013; The Hartman Group, Inc.

2. AC Nielsen Scantrack, xAOC channels, past four years, quad week ending 05/18/2019.

Over and again, the Skate Ramp has allowed CPG innovators to sneak up on arrogant and complacent category leaders—who, by the time they realize what is going on, can't get to market fast enough to block the challenger's growth. They become fast followers, at best. Fingers start pointing. Middle-aged general managers quit to open yoga studios.

The most famous example of a Skate Ramp attack in the last 25 years was Chobani's utter thrashing of the flat-footed yogurt incumbents in the United States market. Even more incredible was that the author of this stunning upset was *not* an Ivy-league educated MBA brand manager with years of brand marketing experience. And, trust me, this was incredibly humbling for general managers in other categories, as well. The faces of executives throughout the industry took on the solemn gaze of funeral attendees whenever the name *Chobani* came up.

A recent, internal study at The Hartman Group determined roughly 70 percent of early-stage, premium food/beverage brands that crossed the nine-figure threshold since the Great Recession of 2008–2009 rode the Skate Ramp all the way.[3] The inference we made at the time is that the Skate Ramp is the growth curve that best predicts a new CPG brand's capability to scale into a middle-market company.

Today, I still believe the Skate Ramp is the competitively advantaged growth model for most entrepreneurial CPG brands. Not the Unicorn ramp. Certainly not the ADA ramp. (Figure 3) This book will uncover what this exponential growth curve reveals about the power of the branded product line driving it.

Another fascinating aspect of the Skate Ramp is that you can mathematically determine if you're on it anytime you'd like, as long you have 18–24 months of rolling quad week point-of-sale (POS) data. You don't need to wait five years and then look in the rear-view mirror.

Around 30–35 percent of premium CPG brands launched each year ride the Skate Ramp for at least their first three years, with an

---

3. This figure is approximate, based on internal Hartman Group research conducted in 2017, using multiple sources of information (Euromonitor 2017; AC Nielsen Scantrack, xAOC channels, past four years, week ending 12/31/2016; and public sources). Analysis courtesy of The Hartman Group, Inc.

Figure 3: Entrepreneurial Growth Paths

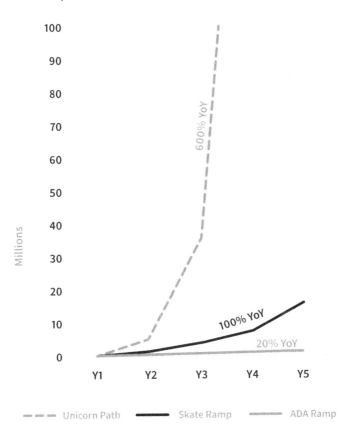

In comparing the Skate Ramp (exponential) growth path with the Unicorn (steep) and Wheelchair (linear) growth paths, it is easy to see which one is the most reasonable, sustainable, and desirable for early-stage CPG brands.

average year-one (Y1) revenue of $134,000.[4] This is a bit misleadingly optimistic, though, because the analysis upon which it is based included brands that grew fast off of a tiny year-one revenue base, and quite frankly, the sample was small (28 of the 72 premium food/beverage brands that launched in 2011).

4. AC Nielsen Scantrack, xAOC+C channels, past five years, week ending 11/21/2015; analysis courtesy of The Hartman Group, Inc.

Staying on this ambitious growth curve gets much more difficult over time. Many brands fall off the Skate Ramp as they grow, much like the newbies who invade the neighborhood skate park and don't make it halfway up the steeper ramps before losing momentum and their balance. That's why only about 10 percent of early-stage premium CPG brands are riding the Skate Ramp at any given time.[5] That's also why, once they leave the giddy early years of launching, only 2 percent of such brands selling between $1 million and $100 million in point-of-sale (POS) revenue are still riding it.[6]

The Ramp is challenging. But you *can* learn to ride it.

Why Chasing Doors Is No Way to Scale

Traditionally, most CPG entrepreneurs have worked with sales consultants and brokers to add account after account as their primary, and often only, growth technique. They manage the company basically like a business-to-business (B2B) operation. There is little contact with the end consumer. Stakeholders in the value chain rarely bring up the end consumer. They are institutionally too focused on managing their mark-up percentages and on tweaking fees and chargebacks to you, the supplier.

Brokers, distributors, and to some extent even retailers are subconsciously aligned on one *key performance indicator* (KPI): absolute case-volume movement. The base income of brokers and distributors is a percentage of the case dollar-volume moved through the supply chain to the shelf. In the short-term, these go-to-market stakeholders have no real incentive to pace growth or to be terribly strategic about it. Any case-volume growth is good growth to the less scrupulous among them.

Although few brokers I've met would promise clients 600 percent YoY growth without a massive pile of slotting cash on hand, and prob-

5. AC Nielsen Scantrack, xAOC+C channels, past five years, week ending 11/21/2015; analysis courtesy of The Hartman Group, Inc.
6. AC Nielsen Scantrack, xAOC+C channels, past five years, week ending 11/21/2015; analysis courtesy of The Hartman Group, Inc.

ably not even then, brokers and distributors are not good-faith advisors to CPG entrepreneurs on what is *reasonably* fast growth. Their position in the value chain makes them a dangerously biased source of primary strategic business advice.

Time and again, new CPG founders have seen large door-count gains the first year only to see their products delisted (dropped by retail buyers) and their topline (gross sales) reduced the next year. I recently worked with a frozen prepared food client with an amazing, on-trend product. A very reputable brokerage firm had led him to a premature national expansion via stacking account after account after account. When shelf velocities fell far below declared minimums, accounts began to delist his brand. By the following year, the brand had lost more than 50 percent of its initial sales volume.

Months before, when the founder told me about the impending national expansion, I had warned him not to aggressively expand until he knew more about his consumer and had developed a multidimensional playbook to create demand. About a year after that conversation, I got a random, out-of-nowhere LinkedIn message from him:

Sam: "You were right, James."
Me: "Hi, Sam. I'm lost. . . . Right about what?"
Sam: "Don't go wide; go deep first."

So, how can CPG entrepreneurs set a reasonably fast growth rate and sustain it?

I have to be honest. In the history of CPG entrepreneurship, stacking accounts on top of each other has worked for many well-known brands on the journey to $10 million. It worked exceptionally well in the 1980s and 1990s, when premium CPG was so new in the United States that many entrepreneurial brands (outside of beer, chocolate, and cheese) had perhaps one national competitor, if any at all. Selling premium CPG products at that time was restricted almost entirely to the natural and specialty channels and through mail order catalogues (often to gift shop owners). For many brands, it was mostly a seasonal, fourth quarter (Q4) market niche. I remember getting Toblerone bars as a fancy-pants, upper middle-class Christmas gift in the 1980s. After the tree went to the dump, we would go back to Hershey bars for the rest of the year.

At the time, there was a significant cap on the potential scale that any premium brand (outside of alcohol) could generate. New brands did not suddenly find themselves in 4,000 stores like they do today, when they agree to unwise trade deals with retailers not fully transparent about their ulterior motives. Those were the glory days of selling premium CPG brands in a purely B2B mode of operations. Aggressive year-round consumer marketing probably wouldn't have worked too well for premium players in that era, when no brand had a sizeable addressable market in any major metropolitan area. If the children of corporate attorneys snap back to Hershey's after tasting Toblerone, you have a real scaling problem.

Today, however, the average value-added grocery category has multiple national premium CPG players. The refrigerated cases of dips, yogurt, bottled water, kombucha, and alternative milks, for example, are filled with literally dozens of nationally distributed premium offerings. In the most saturated categories, you'll also find numerous venture-capital–backed national brands with piles of cash to manipulate consumer demand in their favor.

This creates a two-fold competitive problem for emerging CPG brands in the early journey to seven and eight figures:

How do you grow fast and sustain that growth while facing the potential reaction of better-funded national premium players ahead of you?

The answer is not simply to raise a massive amount of capital. That's because you must first demonstrate strong market performance worthy of a seven-figure raise. Unless you are blessed with an extended family of high net-worth individuals (HNWI), that kind of raise, even from angels, will involve tight scrutiny of your business' top and bottom lines.[7]

Given this, we can see that the CPG entrepreneur's problem complicates further:

How do you grow reasonably fast and sustain that growth while facing the potential reaction of better-funded national premium players and thereby enhance your ability to raise private and institutional capital to fund acceleration?

This complicated challenge sums up what it's like to take the entrepreneurial journey from $0 to $10 million in gross sales (or to roughly $20–25 million in retail sales)—the current point at which you can start attracting broad interest from institutional investors focused on CPG. The ability of individual entrepreneurs (or anyone, for that matter) to accurately predict, at the time of launch, whether they'll get from $0 to $10 million is still extremely low. New CPG brands are highly unstable in terms of retail account security, cash flow, and month-to-month velocities—which look more like an unstable heart rhythm than the sales pattern of a mature business. (Figure 4)

Research conducted by The Hartman Group in 2017 suggests that roughly 80 percent of premium food/beverage brands fail to make it past $1 million in xAOC (eXtended All Outlet Combined) sales, or $400,000–500,000 on the entrepreneurs' books.[8] Premium CPG product lines that reach this level of scale tend to survive but don't

---

7. If you look closely at who is winning big capital raises, you'll see that increasingly it is previously successful entrepreneurs and not starry-eyed newcomers. That is because serial entrepreneurs have industry networks that confer upon them much higher levels of trust than is typically accorded a new, small businessperson. This enhances their access to the trade and makes distribution easier to obtain (though not nearly as easy as for Frito-Lay).

8. AC Nielsen Scantrack, xAOC channels, past two years, week ending 12/31/2016; n = 16,000 food and beverage brands included, multiple food/beverage categories, all temperature states; analysis courtesy of The Hartman Group, Inc. The analysis is inferential, based on marking thresholds where brand counts fall off in a statistically meaningful fashion. Note: xAOC is a Nielsen geography that includes grocery stores, drug stores, Target, all Walmart stores, some Club (no Costco), some military, and major Dollar chains.

Figure 4: Unstable Weekly Velocities of New CPG Brands

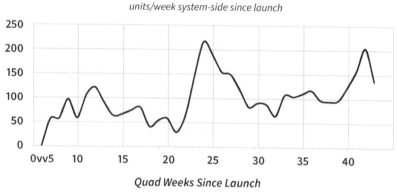

Premium Snack Brand in BigCo Retailer
units/week system-side since launch

Quad Weeks Since Launch

Weekly velocities of premium snack brand in BigCo retailer.[9]

necessarily grow fast enough to ever earn the distribution gains and consumer enthusiasm necessary to continue growing.

Yet, more than 100 premium CPG brands have scaled into mature nine-figure businesses.[10] Surely, there must be similarities in the approaches taken by these brands. Surely, these common practices could be used by other young CPG brands to increase the odds not only of surviving but also of growing sustainably faster than average, despite increasing competitive pressure in the market.

My primary objective in writing this book is to share those common practices with today's CPG entrepreneurs grinding away in the sub-$10 million zone. In these pages you will learn the characteristics, strategies, and techniques that exponential growth brands have used (intentionally or unintentionally) since the Great Recession to go from launch to sustainable growth and nine-figure scale. Brands we all know that are part of this elite Skate Ramp club include Skinny-

9. Premium Growth Solutions client files, blinded to protect the retailer and brand owner.
10. This figure is approximate. Based on internal research conducted by The Hartman Group in 2017 using multiple sources of information (Euromonitor 2017; AC Nielsen Scantrack xAOC, past four years, week ending 12/31/2016; and public sources); analysis courtesy of The Hartman Group, Inc.

And the Skate Ramp Champions Are . . .

For those curious enough to do your own case study research, the following is a partial list of Skate Ramp winners.

Annie's, Bai, Boar's Head, Sanpellegrino, Dave's Killer Bread, GoGo squeeZ, Sensible Portions, Gold Peak Tea, GT's kombucha, Hint, Think!, Harvest Snaps, Honest Tea, Justin's, Talenti, Kind, Kerrygold, Lärabar, Yogi Tea, siggi's, Nature's Bakery, Tate's Bake Shop, La Croix, SkinnyPop, LUNA Bar, noosa, Organicgirl, Pacific Foods, Plum Organics, Pretzel Crisps, Perfect Bar, Sabra, Stacy's, Vita Coco.*

*No doubt, other brands—including several packaged-produce trademarks—also rode this curve, but their data is not available to me.

Pop, Kind, siggi's, Vita Coco, GT's, Sabra, Plum Organics, and Stacy's, among many others.

What I've found is that these companies all shared certain features from very early on, way before they received notoriety or large investment support.[11]

Ride the Ramp Well, Follow the Consumer

In CPG, there are two primary levers of growth: distribution and consumer demand.[12] The *C* in CPG is there for a reason. As most founders who have scaled a CPG business will tell you, if you ignore the consumer in your growth strategy, you are unlikely to scale to anywhere

11. Many frustrated entrepreneurs struggling to raise capital complain that "only businesses that receive large raises ever scale." That is not really true, as tracking the performance of CPG portfolio companies reveals. In fact, venture capitalists are very good at ignoring and writing off their frequently misspent investment capital. What is true is that investment capital can prop up businesses with limited scale potential for 7–10 extra years. But capital alone does not guarantee sustainable growth and lasting scale for CPG entrepreneurs, any more than public companies can expect to sustain a line extension simply by throwing money at every launch. If only it were so easy.
12. Byron Sharp, in *How Brands Grow,* describes distribution as "physical availability" and consumer demand as "mental availability."

near $100 million or to even $25 million. Because, as a CPG business, to maintain any scale you've achieved, you have to generate and sustain repeat purchase. Ramp-ups built entirely on trial (i.e., trying your product once) are a corporate house of cards, blown away by the slightest trade winds.

Really, only retailers can scale branded product lines purely on the basis of distribution (for example, via value or discount private label, because they remove any influence of pricing). If, as a branded good, you focus solely on distribution, you usually wind up with a commodity packaged good. By *commodity* I mean a product purchased not for its uniquely memorable user experience (symbolic or sensory) but simply because it was at the right place at the right time. The product is purchased by some random consumer who happened to need something like it at that moment and had no strong brand preference. When defined this way, a commodity is a product that may have a trademark on the front panel but is essentially forgettable.

Forgettable versus memorable.

This is the fundamental difference between the competitive challenge faced by CPG entrepreneurs ramping a new brand versus a Lay's or Cheerio's launching a new product line or sub-brand. Undercapitalized CPG entrepreneurs must be far more memorable than the average CPG product launch. Unlike BigCo brands, they can't simply buy access to distribution, to immediate mass consumer awareness, or to instant trust. They need to generate repeat sales faster and hold them better, and only superior memorability can make that happen.

Massive trial is the #1 strategic lever that big corporations use to get a (typically not very innovative) product line extension to stick. They do this by throwing large slotting budgets and large advertising campaigns at the launch. They are happy with low levels of annual repeat purchase (typical with BigCo) because they make tons of money on the initial trial itself (unlike you, the CPG entrepreneur). They generate large amounts of trial simply by having prime shelf placement, right next to their trademark's base UPCs. Their launch model is based on having a trusted, well-known trademark on the front panel.

This BigCo growth model is not really about growth at all. It's

what I call a *grab-n-hold* model, because it simply grabs from existing demand, which is based heavily on consumer trust in the sensory
or symbolic experience of a well-known brand. Want protein in your
snack? More folks will trust getting it from Nature Valley or Clif than
from some upstart CPG brand they've never heard of before. This is
the cruel reality that new entrepreneurs have to contend with as they
ramp up.

––––––––––

With this admittedly wonky context in hand, hopefully you can see why
I could not, in good conscience, pretend to work on a plan for unicorn growth with my Arizona client. Twelve months is just not enough
time to magically create consumer awareness and enthusiasm for a new
brand across an entire country as big, fragmented, and complicated as
ours. Nor did my client have the capital to quickly build high levels of
consumer awareness and enthusiasm, which is often the case with new
CPG brands. Their premium soft drink would need to have been one
of those ultra-rare products for which marketing outreach is basically
unnecessary because shoppers are predisposed to its phenomenally
well-timed product symbolism. (More on this in Part One.)

So, why do so many new CPG entrepreneurs fall into the unicorn fantasy when they want to grow fast?

It comes down to naively believing that predisposed shoppers will:

- Simply notice your brand once it appears, and
- Have the same intense reaction to your package symbolism as you do, its authors

I call this the *baby stroller fallacy*. Every mother, as she pushes her
baby down the sidewalk or in the park or through the mall, thinks her
little one is amazing and noteworthy and precious. Every. Single. One.
Yet, to passersby, it's just another baby. Most walk by and don't offer
more than a weak, courteous smile in the face of human fertility.

Nationwide sprint strategies aimed at a BigCo or unicorn growth pace almost always fail for CPG entrepreneurs (or any new brand), due to four factors:

1. Low to no awareness of the trademark (by the trade and by the consumer)[13]

2. Premium price points that immediately eliminate 90 percent or more of category consumers[14]

3. Limited capital to spend on:

    › rapid expansion of distribution (slotting, distributor set-up fees, production ramp costs, etc.),

    › aggressive, immediate, high-impression omni-media advertising.

4. Retailers and distributors can and will easily replace you if something else comes along with better potential and better funding.

As a CPG entrepreneur, you are neither Hershey's with its army of field sales reps nor Coca-Cola North America with its massive fleet of cute red trucks. You are not launching the next cool flavor of Doritos to a nation of consumers who know your brand, the majority of whom have eaten it at least once before. (FYI: Upwards of 75 percent of adults alive today in the United States have eaten Doritos before.)[15]

---

13. Premium Growth Solutions, 2019 Premium Brand Awareness surveys; June 2019, n = 1,000 adults. Awareness levels of fast-growing brands are generally well below 10%, in the mid-to-low single digits of the adult population.

14. Premium Growth Solutions analysis; June 2019; n = 1000 adults. Based on a survey of randomly selected grocery categories from Nielsen's 2019 AOD taxonomy in which consumers were asked if they would pay 50%+ more per item in the randomly chosen categories. The median percentage who would pay more was 8.4%. Fresh fruit scored the highest, which should not surprise anyone, given that it is one of the top categories for organic purchasing and has a strong socio-cultural function in the American diet.

15. Premium Growth Solutions survey; June 2019; n = 500 adults.

In fact, there are virtually no instances of distribution prowess alone driving explosive growth anywhere in consumer-packaged goods. Not even the most successful new brands launched by public firms in the past 25 years used distribution and only distribution to scale, even though they have the best access to it in the world.[16] Not DiGiorno pizza in 1995. Not Activia yogurt in 2006 (U.S. launch). Not Magnum ice cream in 2011 (U.S. launch). Even Chobani's phenomenally fast growth from 2005–2010 cannot be explained purely on the basis of manipulating distribution.[17]

Instead of acting like BigCo, CPG entrepreneurs have to work with the known advantages they do have—namely:

- When looking for new consumers, your brand is a blank cultural slate and has no baggage to deal with.

- Retailers want premium-priced growth brands to attract affluent shoppers (who spend more), to boost department profits, and/or to boost their brand image.

- You are nimble, scrappy, and can make bold decisions very quickly when necessary.

- You offer premium-quality goods (if you're like most entrepreneurial CPG brands today). That means, once you've reached initial viable scale, your chance of achieving long-term viability is much higher than Kraft's latest line extension (for which even they secretly hold out little hope).[18]

---

16. Many CPG sales executives have fallen on their faces claiming they would be the one to make distribution move an R&D turd.

17. "The Rise of Greek," 03/22/2011, UBS, Figure 20. In this widely published in-depth analysis of Chobani's take-over of the yogurt category, UBS Investment used Nielsen data to show Chobani had high, stable velocities as it ramped its distribution from 10–52%, Max ACV in xAOC channels. This is a classic sign of demand-driven growth or consumer pull.

18. AC Nielsen Scantrack, xAOC+C, past five years, week ending 11/21/2015; analysis of a random sample of 700 premium brands in 42 different categories; analysis courtesy of the Hartman Group, Inc. As premium CPG brands reach about $7 million in POS sales, on average, their chances of declining drop to 11% or less.

I cannot stress enough the importance of memorability in scaling a young CPG brand. New CPG entrepreneurs must work insanely hard to create and promote a highly memorable product experience. Memorability is the primary strategic advantage you have, and it is critical to sustaining your ride on the Skate Ramp.

It would be easy to deem exponential growth too hard and settle for linear growth or stagnation. *Hey, at least I'm still in business,* you might say to yourself. But those who choose to follow the lead of Skate Ramp brands will be rewarded with:

- Robust, growing velocities

- More leverage with the retail trade because of those velocities

- Better shelf placement and depth

- The ability to create entirely new categories with the trade

- Strong cash flow

- Higher gross profits per unit

- The ability to attract strong interest from top investors who can fund key activities at the appropriate times

In the following chapters I share what I've learned by studying the brands that made it not only past $500,000 and past $10 million but all the way past $100 million along the exponential Skate Ramp growth curve. You've already met several members of that elite club in this Introduction. These brands can ride!

First, an Important Message from the Author

Before we delve into what sets Skate Ramp brands apart from other new CPG brands, I encourage you to read the following housekeeping statements, so you don't move forward with the wrong expectations.

The principles I outline in this book do not foster exponential growth equally well in all CPG categories. This is primarily due to four factors:

1. Some categories exhibit a culturally predetermined lack of demand for premium priced goods.

2. Some categories exhibit a very long purchase cycle (and low purchase volume) that makes quickly bringing a new brand into a consumer's rotating set of preferred brands very problematic in a crowded CPG marketplace.

3. Some categories are caged in by holiday-buying assumptions that dramatically limit off-season trial of premium-priced goods.

4. In the case of the latter two items (low buy rates and limiting holiday-buying assumptions), distribution plays an outsized role in the growth process.

This is not an operations manual or a ten-step tactical playbook to generate exponential growth. Every CPG startup team must create their own, market-tested playbook in the real world. This book is designed to teach you how to think about exponential growth strategy. There is no comprehensive master playbook of tactics that can guarantee you will magically ride the Skate Ramp to glory. This book coaches you on how to think like a world-class growth strategist and shares some of the best practices commonly executed by Skate Ramp brands. It teaches you to learn from specific shared behavior of Skate Ramp winners that I can analytically connect to consumer behavior—including behavior that even founders may have been unaware of as they executed. A correlation between a "best practice" and a specific business is worthless unless that correlation can be explained by human behavioral rules. Correlations without a why are strategically worthless. You must co-create your own individual playbook with your early consumers. There is just no way around this.

Scaling any entrepreneurial CPG brand at exponential (but not unicorn) rates always involves a lot of grit and sheer luck. Anyone who has raised large amounts of seed capital knows what I'm talking about. If this book could eliminate the luck component entirely, I'd charge a hell of a lot more for it than I am.

This is not a marketing science textbook. Yes, the growth-contributing variables behind thousands of $100 million and up CPG brands can be statistically separated out and analyzed for relative significance. However, not enough premium brands have scaled to that degree (yet) to conduct a truly meaningful data science experiment. Reverse-engineering the many variables contributing to the successful scaling of premium brands is also still open to interpretation and debate.

And those thousands of other CPG brands I mentioned earlier? Almost all are actually late-stage brands whose ramp-up happened decades ago and therefore are beyond the reach of our data grasps. Contrary to what some marketing scientists contend, neither analyzing international ramp-up case studies, data science, nor calculus equations can really help us understand why Oreo, Lay's, Dove, and so on ramped up the way they did. Nor does it matter, because their era of ramp-up is long gone.

This book is written specifically for premium CPG entrepreneurs who are new to the industry and particularly for those ambitious founders who are hellbent on beating the odds and riding the Skate Ramp to scale. That said, the principles I explain in these pages will be of interest to anyone in the broader food and beverage industries, especially those running low-budget incubators, garages, and ventures groups inside strategic giants.

This book is meant to save you the time and energy of learning best practices on your own. And while the data in this book comes from food and beverage brands, I have seen most of the principles operative in personal care, home care, pet food and other CPG verticals. It is also meant to give you a truly independent perspective on all the various stakeholders you will encounter. I guarantee that no class of stakeholder will read this book without feeling miffed. This is where the real-life evidence has taken me, though. And I believe you, the founder, should have a more transparent view of the industry you are operating in. I am here to help, not make friends.

I use mixed methodologies. I have no allegiance to any angle of execution in CPG, and so you will see me discuss all sorts of data: direct, inferential, structured, unstructured, quant heavy, quant lite. Ultimately, I agree with a statement Jeff Bezos made during a 2018 speaking event: "The thing I have noticed is [that] when the anecdotes and the data disagree, the anecdotes are usually right. There's something wrong with the way you are measuring it."[19] This book uses quantitative data where it adds strategic insight, not where it blinds founders to reality. I used to consult for public companies who relied so heavily on quantitative datasets to drive decisions (inciting endless arguments and political jockeying) that they lost the ability to intuit anything about the market or their consumers. Data serves *you*, not the other way around.

Finally, you may want to note that I am a social scientist as well as a business strategist. This means I believe that changing individual eating behavior is primarily a social process and one that takes much more effort than most people realize, especially the over-eager entrepreneur.

In the food/beverage arena, for example, individual dietary inertia for the average American is remarkable when it is dispassionately analyzed. (Any registered dietician would be happy to support me here, backed by their patient files, I'm sure.) This is especially true when it comes to getting consumers to add multiple premium CPG products to their weekly repertoire. That is why it is so important to target your offering in dense social networks of consumers that are inclined to want your product.

The flip side of our dietary stubbornness is that we humans are remarkably insecure beings. We crave social conformity and interaction. Our brains evolved to engage in complex affinities with others.

---

19. 04/21/2018. https://www.businessinsider.com/bezos-explains-his-dreaded-one-character-emails-2018-4

In fully realized consumer economies like that of the United States, we will literally purchase things to fit in or to tell a public story about who we are. We will change our diet (or baby care or beauty regimen or other habit), in part, to keep up with our friends. If premium goods are important to our friends, we will slowly (or not so slowly) adopt them in order to remain connected.

This is the reality of a consumer society. Our social lives and mental well-being are driven more by our consumption habits than by our inherited identities or pre-modern status markers.

At points in this book, I encourage founders to acknowledge these fundamental social science truths in their strategic planning. If they do, they will outperform those who simply stand at trade show booths and dream of missions fulfilled.

PART ONE

DESIGNING TO
COMMAND A PREMIUM

PHASE 1 $0–$1M

CHAPTER 1

WHY SMARTER DESIGN
IS SO CRITICAL

very year, hundreds of young CPG brands publish founder narratives in order to gain general credibility and to attract investor funding. Most of these stories focus on the founder's mission or purpose. Yet, those are not the tales that should intrigue us. Rather, we should focus on the stories about how the founders came up with their novel product. After all, don't we admire innovators in consumer packaged goods primarily for their visionary creations?

As I wrote this chapter, I stumbled upon the following product-origin narrative for a product line trademarked Your Super:

As chemotherapy sapped [her boyfriend's] energy level day by day, de Groot struggled with seeing him suffer. That's when the health-food guru inside her sprang into action. With the help of her aunt, an orthomolecular nutritionist—one who specializes in dietary supplements—she dug into various bags of vitamin-rich "super grains" in her kitchen and began a strict smoothie cleanse for Kuech. And he actually started to feel better—more alert and energized, de Groot, now 28, says.[20]

---

20. Talib Visram, "They Met on the Tennis Court. Now, This Couple Is Serving Up Supple-

I have no idea what an orthomolecular nutritionist is, but I get the strong sense, as I imagine you do, that this is a person who knows the supplement space cold. No doubt they know it even better than most supplement store owners. Kristel de Groot created her innovation by combining the domain expertise of a professional, her aunt, with her own experimental intuition.

Whether Your Super's formulas are 100 percent distinct in the supplement category is less important to my point here than the fact that the intent was to innovate beyond the catalogue of known offerings. The founder couldn't find what she was seeking and so got to work inventing it.

When we come across these kinds of product-origin narratives in trade media, what should we make of them? Although some are clearly dressed-up promotional pieces, the intent to innovate displayed in these stories is the real crucible of exponential growth in CPG.

The problem is that as founders are doing their product development, they don't have access to a science-based, publicly available formula for the kind of product design that facilitates exponential growth. They innovate with pure intent but primarily with knowledge gleaned from the margins of science and medicine and from the broader food culture.

In fact, if you walk the halls of Expo West with an eye toward CPG product design, you will notice very quickly that this is not a show built around design excellence. That's the irony of today's trade shows geared toward emerging CPG brands. They're built more on passionate *intent* than on brilliant *execution* (i.e., the "hope" in New Hope). But that is to be expected when booths are filled largely with outsiders to a complex, consumer-facing industry.

So, how can founders improve their design IQ such that they can design better product lines, ones with the best potential for becoming exponential growers? What are the key variables to experiment with in order to design products that generate above-average levels of memorability—and rapidly.

---

ments–and Their Superfood Company Is Thriving," *Inc.* magazine, April 18, 2019.

I will address these questions in Part One, though one could easily write an entire book on them. That's how important they are for founders who want to ride the Skate Ramp.

————————

The case for smarter CPG product design presented in Chapters 1 through 4 is based upon some common industry knowledge—which, to my continued frustration, is not well-known among most CPG entrepreneurs. Having a solid grasp of these fundamental principles is critical to understanding and applying more advanced design principles that correlate with long-term exponential growth (i.e., riding the Ramp).

The most central assumption underlying consumer products and everything in this book is that *consumers shop categories.* Retailers also manage categories.

Categories are culturally shared linguistic/cognitive handles used across CPG stakeholder groups. We may quibble about each other's definitions, and not all category taxonomies line up beautifully, but categories remain critical cognitive tools for connecting with consumers. In fact, when stakeholders disagree on the category in which a product fits, you must *always* side with the consumer. Not the buyer. Not the distributor. Not your own team. Not your investors.

In order to grow well, new CPG brands need to find a category-specific foothold (regardless of how they source their revenue volume). Therefore, category-based innovation is everything as you go to market in CPG. Too often I encounter newer, highly idealistic entrepreneurs who think they are selling the consumer a mission, or worse, a platform, and then treat category as some lagging variable, like flavor or pack size.

One passionate, first-year founder declared to me, "I want to own [Name of Magical Commodity] in every aisle in the grocery store!" That kind of thinking misplaces ego for strategy. All successful CPG innovation is category-based, including innovation that introduces a new category.[21]

The following three strategic-growth principles for early-stage CPG brands rest on the assumption that category is everything in CPG strategy. Newcomers often view these core principles as being sufficient for sustainable growth. But *core* doesn't mean *end all*. In reality, even these three core principles together are insufficient in today's oversaturated market.

Premium: What's Growing Best in CPG

Since the Great Recession, premium product lines (i.e., perceived higher quality than the category norm at a unit-price premium) have been the primary engine of growth in today's United States CPG marketplace.[22] And, let's face it, premium brands represent the vast majority of entrepreneurial CPG brands in play at the moment. While a few old-school processed brands are still launching every once in a while, these are virtually all produced by mid- to large-scale companies (e.g., Takis extruded snacks, Mio water enhancers, Devour frozen meals, etc.). Only BigCo can create scale fast enough to make money at the low-average unit prices the target audience of these product lines demands.

If it's new in CPG today, we're basically talking about what used to be called the *natural products industry*.[23] I use the term *premium* instead of *natural* for three reasons:

---

21. From a cultural perspective, there is no such thing as a "new category," because even the most obscure foreign food item will be framed through an indigenous consumer category taxonomy, including by retailers. This is what happened to hummus in the 1990s. Not until it became a major, multi-brand segment of dips did folks start to see it as its own phenomenon. Likewise, moving an existing category, like protein bars, into a different temperature state is less a cultural shift in category than a shift in planogram. Therefore, although the Perfect Bar did not confuse consumers, it did cause retailers some concern, leading to structural delays in its ramp up.

22. Euromonitor, 2019. Recent analysis courtesy of The Hartman Group, Inc. This analysis is skewed toward nine-figure and up businesses only. Mainstream, legacy-branded packaged food and beverage brands had a median four-year $ CAGR of 1% from 2009–2018. Premium brands, however, exhibited a median growth rate of 11% during the same period.

23. "Natural products" is not a separate industry, despite what certain organizations will have

1. The product lines in question are almost always trading at a per-unit price premium versus the category unit-price average.

2. They are selling formulations that offer non-standard, modern product attributes and sensory experiences (even if barely) to the end consumer.

3. In consumer packaged goods, waving an organic wand or other forms of formula de-processing are no longer enough to attain and sustain scale. (More on this in Chapter 3.)

New Is Not Enough

Each of the four major retail trade shows for natural products is followed by a flurry of trend lists from agencies, trendwatchers, media pundits, etc. I've studied these lists, and if you do it systematically, you will notice something odd. The "trending" premium product symbolism (claims, magical ingredients, diet trends du jour) cited on these lists seem to overlap show to show and year to year, while the brands featured as examples constantly rotate. Hmmm.

This suggests the power of the authors' subjective fixations, but more importantly, it also suggests the startling fact that something as obscure as prebiotic food or forgotten beverages like switchel could feature multiple brands in today's marketplace. It is an indirect measure of something trade show operators will tell you privately: the intense level of launching going on in CPG today.

In fact, the New Products Hall at Expo West is really a fertility temple for the modern CPG industry. Folks are super pumped at these

---

you believe. It's a segment within almost every CPG category for sale today. The reason some consider it an industry is that for decades it required a separate co-manufacturing, distribution, and retail ecosystem in order to get anything to market. The major players wouldn't work with tiny companies, like Annie's, Stonyfield, and Horizon. That is no longer true. Today, most co-manufacturers can make these products. Large distributors like McLane also happily work with natural products, and natural products are sold in dollar stores, ALDI, even Grocery Outlet.

booths, like many first-time mothers I've met. They're the opposite of the jaded sales dudes I see at Sweets and Snacks.

Yet, the high failure rate of new CPG brands should serve as an early warning to ambitious innovators that a new offering is not by itself sufficient to create the exponential growth exhibited by the elite club of Skate Ramp brands discussed in the introduction of this book. It isn't even enough to guarantee survival in the journey to the first $500,000 in gross sales, especially in brick-and-mortar launches.

Over the years, the CPG industry has witnessed hundreds of historically new premium innovations that are substantively different in their respective categories on a national level. Vitamin-enhanced water. Kale chips. Aloe (in juice). Hummus. Za'atar (in condiments). Kombucha. Pita chips. Greek yogurt. The best ones have introduced entirely new segments within existing categories; some have even calved off as separate trade categories. Yet, as you can already tell from my list of examples, not all of these innovations generated either exponential growth or scale to a degree that transforms the market. Aloe juice and kale chips refuse to scale no matter how much capital is thrown at them. Rhythm Superfoods, the best-funded kale chip brand to date, has had to diversify well beyond kale in order to grow. Za'atar is an unwritten story so far. Hang on to find out.

More importantly, each of the successful innovations among those I just mentioned—vitamin-enhanced water, kombucha, hummus, pita chips, and Greek yogurt—ramped up to scale on very different timelines. (More to come on why this is true.) It's too easy, therefore, to predict newcomer za'atar a failure in condiments, for example, because the early brands have not yet taken off. That's what pita chips looked like in 1995, hummus in 1998, and Greek yogurt in 2000. Too often I see investors writing off new innovations because they haven't found a fast-growing brand yet. As I'm about to explain, first movers in CPG, especially premium CPG, don't always have their go-to-market act together, because they are usually industry outsiders.

First Movers Nationally Don't Always Win

Not only is being first to the national marketplace not always enough to scale, but neither is it enough to create exponential growth in a new food/beverage innovation (e.g., Greek yogurt). Chobani, after all, was the second Greek yogurt brand to go national in the United States—not the first, which was FAGE, in 1998. Athenos was first to distribute packaged hummus nationally in the United States (and in conventional channels), as early as 1999,[24] but Sabra was the first to scale a national hummus line, in the late 2000s.

The problem with many national first-movers in premium CPG is that the low barrier to initial entry (into independent stores, specifically) means that the first to the national market is often an inexperienced entrepreneur without industry knowledge, without a strong network of industry experts, and without ready access to financing.[25] Or they are sold by sleepy, specialty food manufacturers comfortable with the closed-in, predictable confines of the specialty foods channel. In some cases, they prefer to remain *special* and *rare*. Not understanding the power of retail channels (or trade classifications) also causes many new-timers to view mass retailers like Target, for example, as equivalent or superior to a local Kroger chain with one-tenth the store count, a judgment founded solely on optimistic case-volume projections based on the chains' relative store counts.

These handicaps don't necessarily kill the viability of an entrepreneurial brand. However, they do make them less able to react swiftly to more empowered copycats (or independently coincidental innovators) and less able to competently expand nationally and remain in distribution. That can effectively prohibit them from ever reaching scale and/or from capturing a significant share of premium sales avail-

---

24. https://issuu.com/jewishpress7/docs/2000-09-29, p. 66; the earliest online mention of the brand. Athenos never scaled due to a common CPG malaise: trying to platform healthy specialty foods within a lifestyle brand (Mediterranean) and lost focus (feta cheese, yogurt, pita chips, etc.). Athenos was once part of Kraft's specialty cheese division, an acquired company called Churny.
25. In the case of FAGE, it came down to a refusal to properly adapt the Greek pack design to an unfamiliar cultural market like the United States and a pessimistic view of the upside in general. The FAGE Total pack of 1998 is a textbook case of poor branding and pack design.

able in the category quickly enough to sustain their scale. Undercapitalized and inexperienced brands easily get stuck in or snap back into marginal, low-scale channels, while others beat them to the higher traffic supermarket locations.

In today's market, it is also incredibly easy for a better-positioned serial entrepreneur to beat you to scale with the trade. This level of leapfrogging is only growing as trade shows actively encourage heavy media coverage on the show floor, which overexposes high-potential innovations to a massive internet audience, including strategics (i.e., large CPG companies that acquire early-stage brands) and corporate venture capitalists. Pitch slams, too, have become easy ways for the seasoned to learn about new innovations and to copy the ideas of inexperienced, giddy innovators. I have personally verified three instances where wealthier serial entrepreneurs have relatively easily copied the young innovator's idea and outflanked them. You may have your own stories.

In sum, premium offerings that are new to the world or even first to national distribution don't miraculously create long-term competitive advantage. Your product design must have some built-in magic and built-in defenses to give you the lead time to scale and to stay there. Entrepreneurial passion is just no longer enough in consumer packaged goods. As I'll show in the next few chapters, it takes a specific kind of newness or innovation to generate exponential growth—and only after you apply other best practices.

The key to designing a brand destined for the Skate Ramp is a deep, near obsessive immersion in a specific category of food and beverage. If today's founders would focus as much on their category and how they are innovating within it as they do about their purpose and mission, Expo West could essentially replace the tired innovation approaches still used by many teams at BigCo.

CHAPTER 2

THINK SMARTER ABOUT VALIDATION

You may have heard the term *product-market fit* in your networking journey.[26] I have to admit, it's the clunkiest piece of business jargon I've ever encountered. Marcus Andreesen may be a smart tech investor, but he ain't no poet. I hear new folks to CPG use this techie phrase all the time, even though I've never used it once in my consulting career.

Product-market fit suggests we're about to confront some kind of overly left brain, engineering puzzle—square pegs seeking square holes. A one-time insertion. Yawn. Never has a tech-bro phrase communicated so little of what it is desperately trying to express.

Investors love to toss around product-market fit (as they do brand) as a form of linguistic chest-beating. "We've totally got product-market fit." In this case, the jargon is meant to lull the listener into believing that what follows is a well thought out understanding of why an innovation has the potential to scale to lofty heights.

Far too often, stakeholders with little experience studying the con-

---

26. http://bokardo.com/archives/origin-product-market-fit/

35

sumer adoption of new CPG brands (premium or not) develop their own approaches to determining whether consumers have, in fact, adopted a new CPG brand. Investors and promotional agencies tend to dominate this conversation. Yet, neither knows much about human behavior that well qualifies them to figure this out on their own. In fact, both investors and promotional agencies have a direct incentive to validate a product line optimistically and sloppily, because it increases the number of potential clients and the likelihood of pleasing their existing clients.

Validating a CPG product line generally gets reduced to one of two things:

1. Establishing the line's unique point of differentiation, or
2. Generating strong initial sales velocities

Unique Point of Differentiation

This approach is popular with most run-of-the-mill agencies, who over-promote the value of a product's uniqueness or artistic differentiation via package design and messaging (think "unique selling proposition"). Focusing on the unique point of differentiation makes sense when generating memorable ads for boring commodities, for which the product itself does little of the work. Lean on a bizarre story, over-fund it, and hang on.

Unsurprisingly, this approach to validating a new product line can be very compelling to CPG founders with a creative side. After all, founders want promotional partners to validate how awesome their line is, and words like *unique* and *different* sound validating and ennobling in a nation of snowflakes. Don't they?

The problem is, CPG founders need to design their products for competitive advantage, not for absolute uniqueness (i.e., excessive difference). In this context, the term competitive advantage refers to a strategically executed difference that is competitively scalable. Founders need just enough difference from larger, established players (premium and processed). Finding a unique point of differentiation very easily becomes a navel-gazing artistic exercise, detached both from consumers and from sound business principles.

The marketplace is filled with tons of "unique" CPG products (e.g., juice with chia seeds) that literally have no competitors at all and wouldn't scale even if Mark Cuban sold the Mavericks to fund their growth. Walk the halls of Expo West even once, and I think you'll agree. Here's the hitch: the more unique a product is, the more likely it is simply weird and obscure from the perspective of cultural symbolism and consumer interest. Remember Sahale Snack's Valdosta almond mix? Huh? Weird and obscure don't scale in CPG regardless of promotional efforts—unless those promotional efforts can cleverly mask the weirdness with more accessible symbolism (not a task I would hand the average agency). Yet, if you hang with the ultra-differentiation agency crowd, they will easily take a potentially scalable proposition and cover it up with a jacket made of 100 percent biodynamic Weird.

The seductiveness of being super unique is that rarity is often quite memorable. I'll never forget when I first drank aloe juice and first ate kale chips. Never. Ever. I wish I could forget both. The memorability of the rare is why the local news discusses every twisted murder in your local area, which has nothing to do with local homicide trends. We humans are simply infatuated with anomalous social signals, because our brains are evolved to notice anomalous social threats and to make complex evaluations of social trust. And agencies are paid, ultimately, to gain attention for your brand.

In the CPG industry, however, rarity in its purest form—rare ingredients, rare flavors, rare sensory textures, rare symbols, and rare consumer benefits—is *not* the kind of memorability CPG entrepreneurs want to rely on. That kind of rarity is just weird. And weird is a total black hole of money in CPG innovation. (More to come on why that is so.)

Strong Sales Velocities

Sales velocity—the measure of how quickly a product moves from re-tail shelves to consumer shopping bags—is the math finance folks like to use to validate a new CPG product line. Instead of all art (design/storytelling), it's all data. Yet, it is common for sub-$1 million CPG brands in major CPG categories to initially show strong velocities and velocity growth at tiny scale, only to have sales velocities flatten out and refuse to move, even after increased distribution.

I am continually shocked at how many premium brands grow with investor cash to $10 million or even $20 million without being able to sustain velocity growth in existing stores. The Nielsen/IRI data doesn't lie, folks. If you can't fix your velocity-growth problem at that level of scale, you will have no other choice but to buy distribution to grow. This is expensive and risky. It reminds me too much of the Big-Co launch model—you know, the one that repeatedly leads to product lines that fail and get delisted in two years or less.

The CPG market in the United States is more than capable of ab-sorbing hundreds of permanently niche (i.e., sub-$10 million) offerings with minimal scale potential, especially under the broad frame of "ar-tisan and local brands." In fact, highly unique innovations seem to do this quite frequently when they launch in specialized channels, where consumers are open to and actively seeking the next new thing. In pre-mium health foods, for example, a kind of faddish trial is exhibited by:

- Consumers who are coincidentally converting to a health-ier diet at any given moment due to well-known health triggers (e.g., pregnancy, training for a marathon, cardiac diagnosis, diabetes onset, etc.)

- Health-food geeks who are always looking for the next best thing to bring into their dietary repertoire (to prop up their status as influencers and because they're terrified of missing out on the latest wonder).[27]

---

27. Likewise, foodie fads drive lots of sales in the specialty food channel, where the next home

The great divide between purely quantitative (data) and purely qualitative (artistic) approaches to validating one's product line in CPG is a continuing problem in early-stage growth strategies and with much of the advice circulating at trade events. Ultimately, it is a false distinction that betrays disciplinary biases that don't concern you, the founder. But you absolutely do need to transcend these stakeholder biases. You will encounter them everywhere you go.

What most refer to as product-market fit is really just an awkward investor phrase that corresponds to something much simpler. That is, know your category and where it's headed. Then, design something that can scale competitively within that cultural context, hopefully, reframing consumer understanding of that category over time.

Know your damn category, folks.

It's how your consumer thinks. It's one of the universal variables, like topline sales. You ultimately need to be more of an expert on your category than any buyer you meet. You should be able to embarrass your buyer with your category knowledge.

Yet, many entrepreneurs I meet spend far less time than they should looking at the broader category context in which they sell *before* they design their product and launch. Post-launch, they spend even less time learning from their early consumers in order to figure out whether they are the next aloe juice or the next Greek yogurt. This is critically important to do before you start raising large amounts of money and hit the gas pedal. Sometimes, your first innovation is not the one you should even attempt to scale. Sometimes, it really is your artisan passion. Don't be afraid to start over. Writers, painters, and poets do it all the time. Why not CPG innovators?

More commonly, CPG founders, spend six months or more on product development, followed by a frenzy of selling their product lines based on shallow to no real-world consumer knowledge.[28] Speed is great, but some best practices in product validation should be de-

---

party requires something new to impress and for friends to savor.

28. Many public CPG firms have the opposite problem: teams trying in vain to analyze away most of the risk of a product launch through what can only be described as a massive, bureaucratic attack of *analy-eze*. I once listened to a chief growth officer assign an internal innovation

ployed *prior to acceleration*. Otherwise, ill-informed retail buyers aided by unscrupulous brokers will be happy to take your money and humor your dreams of scale. A whole lot of money. There is no money-back guarantee in CPG.

Yes, it is possible to scale to $1 million without a deep understanding of your category as both a marketplace and a cultural phenomenon. However, understanding your category early on will hasten the refinement of your proposition. It will also minimize wasted capital spent chasing an idea whose potential is permanently niche (i.e., kale chips) versus one that has the potential to capture significant market share over the near and/or long term (Chobani, Halo Top, Kettle, SkinnyPop, etc.).

The tendency to skip over the process of becoming a category expert stems from multiple cultural forces within the entrepreneurial CPG industry today. Chief among those are entrepreneurial romance, the bravado of brokers and less-than-transparent sales consultants, the false logics promoted by inexperienced agencies chasing investor cash, and misdirected founder ego.

So, how do today's CPG founders gain a deep understanding of their category and get a more objective handle on what makes a scalable premium line?

In an attempt to answer this massive question, in the next chapter I introduce four lesser-known laws of new brand growth that have been deployed by many Skate Ramp CPG brands that scaled in the past decade.

---

project to a subordinate with the phrase, "And let's just invite who we need . . . like fifteen people, not fifty." He wasn't joking.

CHAPTER 3

ADVANCED DESIGN PRINCIPLES

f the key to exponential growth and long-term scale in CPG is intense memorability, these five premium CPG design principles are central to creating it:

1. The Law of N+1 Design
2. The Law of High-Stakes Consumer Outcomes
3. The Law of the Attribute-Outcome Symbolism
4. The Law of Formulation Anchoring
5. The Power of Focus, or the Law of Frito-Lay

Each of these key laws of early-stage growth focuses on you, the founder, becoming an obsessive category expert and designing a product experience that will scale fast, largely, if not exclusively, on the merits of your product's sensory experience, its package symbolism, and the word of early consumers.

The Law of N+1 Design

The Boston Consulting Group made the term *trade up* famous in the 2000s, using it to describe the growing consumer trend of switching from mainstream brands to premium and luxury brands.[29] In commodity CPG categories (e.g., produce, meat, eggs, cooking oils, milk, etc.),[30] you can now see 100 percent permanent switching to premium alternatives. For example, I've yet to meet someone who switched intentionally to organic bananas and blueberries and then switched back.[31]

However, in most value-added, processed food/beverage categories, consumers generally don't buy premium brands exclusively on the basis of something being purer and "naturally" formulated, organic or otherwise. (Defined here according to the standard required by WFM and, by default, its primary distributor, UNFI).[32] Indeed, in most categories, a merely natural offering has been distributed nationally for years, across multiple channels. Premium offerings today need to convince consumers that new, more modern symbols and sensory experiences in a category are now socially required on specific eating and drinking occasions.

I call this the *Law of N+1* in premium product design. N+1 = natural + something else.

Assigning social imperatives to a new product line is a moral argument at its core. It is why founders believe their products are "better" than and "superior" to their incumbents. Language is powerful and not accidental in the case of premium CPG.

The primary rhetorical device that conveys socially "required" in our rapidly changing food culture is the broad concept of health and wellness.[33] If you tag a food or beverage product or a brand as "healthier than X," you have what is known in linguistics as a *loaded frame*.[34]

29. Michael Silverstein, Neil Fiske, and John Butman. *Trading Up: The New American Luxury* (Portfolio, 2005).
30. These are commodities because little to no processing is performed on the original farm item.
31. Organic produce buying is based primarily on a belief that harmful chemicals are applied to conventional equivalents. Consumers with that mindset don't wake up and forget about the harmful chemicals. Organic produce also tends to have more intense flavor due to the better soil quality of small producers.
32. See the list of ingredients Whole Foods does not allow here: https://bit.ly/2Lw2d5P
33. In smaller, urban-educated social circles, the concept of 'foodie' becomes a required element of restaurant and dinner party experiences. Foodie experiences involving CPG items are much harder to find. Restaurants still dominate the cultural conversation here.
34. For a more in-depth discussion about linguistic framing, consult the work of Professor

Predisposed listeners will take the statement as probably true until proven otherwise.[35] A much larger group committed to the old way of eating in the category will vehemently reject the statement as "Left Coast bullsh$t." Such is the complex society we live in.

Other loaded frames are at work in the premium CPG marketplace, but for the sake of brevity, I'll focus on the most monetizable ones. Those are: "healthier than" and "better for you." In Chapter 4, I go into greater depth on how to select attributes that can become morally imperative and compelling.

The Law of High-Stakes Consumer Outcomes

In the Introduction, I explained the statistical and strategic folly of planning for unicorn levels of explosive growth in any CPG startup. Even when you're Lance Collins. All praise Lance.

But we're going to ride some unicorns, anyway. Examining a tiny group of CPG unicorns that have appeared since the Great Recession gives us an extreme case study set with which to easily recognize a few key principles behind the design of most of the fast-growing Skate Ramp brands I've studied.

As a cultural anthropologist, I am a fierce proponent of using cultural extremes to shed light on forces of potential change within any society. This belief is based on an old ethnographic field technique used by many of my peers in academia to understand a culture's core value system, but it is also valuable in studying patterns of change within any human-driven domain. This technique rests on empirically validated social-science cases in which, say, weed-enhanced California surf dudes are actually far better sources of information on the core values of suburban middle-class mothers than those mothers are themselves. The marginalized are more insightful on the values of the dominant majority, because they either have rejected those values or

---

George Lakoff. https://georgelakoff.com/tag/framing/

35. A more ominous example of the same linguistic law is when someone accuses another of pedophilic behavior or child endangerment. Many of us will actually believe those kinds of loaded frames until proven false. The risk of it being true is too horrible to wait for proof.

cannot adopt them due to prejudice placed on them, or both. When studying micro-societal change (e.g., transition to natural and organic products at the household level), it is the extreme change agents who can offer far better perspective on (a) what is being changed and (b) what comprises compelling change.

Wait. Don't statistics professors tell you to remove the outliers before running any analysis? Yes, they do. Statistical analysis is all about identifying quantitative trends that are indicative of the core of a measurable phenomenon. Examples of variables where you want to measure the core include top-line growth, velocity, profitability trends, and optimal promotional discount percentages in a category. This is how you *should* think when analyzing your brand's overall performance. You need to anchor the diagnosis of your business on its core performance measures, not by staring at your marginal UPCs or retail accounts or selling territories.

Yet, it is virtually impossible to learn best practices in growth by studying the average entrepreneurial CPG brand, because the average CPG startup is not growing well or at all.[36] The average CPG startup simply makes too many suboptimal decisions that distort the optimal growth-promoting behaviors with signal noise. Some are just lousy products by anyone's estimation. As I said earlier, data science that looks at median or average findings is a waste of computing power for what I'm discussing. It is far more analytically efficient and scientifically valuable to select out the high-performing cases and to first do basic pattern analysis to determine what they have in common that can reasonably be inferred (if not proven) as causal, using available behavioral theory.

The risk in what I'm doing here is that some CPG founders will now believe they are doomed because their product line doesn't follow the exact design of the brands in question. In that event, remem-

---

36. AC Nielsen Scantrack, Total U.S., xAOC+C channels, past four years, random sample of 700 premium brands in 42 different categories, 2011–2015, week ending 11/21/15. Analysis courtesy of The Hartman Group, Inc. Looking at the average YoY growth rate for premium food/beverage brands during the prior three years, the median of these brand averages was *below* the growth rate of the natural/organic sector as a whole.

ADVANCED DESIGN PRINCIPLES   **45**

ber the statement in the Introduction of this book that warns of the ultra-low probability of a new CPG brand pulling off the growth rate of any unicorn.[37] Unicorns are primarily the result of perfect category selection, perfect initial product design, and super lucky market-timing.

With this preamble, I'd like to discuss two recent unicorns: Halo Top and Caulipower. Both feature symbolic communication dynamics common to Skate Ramp brands (several of which are featured throughout the book). Both have also received substantial trade and media attention.

What can we learn from these two media-darling unicorns?

To cut to the main point of this chapter, the meteoric rise of these two upstart brands demonstrates how symbols tied to established, high-stakes dietary needs within broader food culture can drive above-average growth for a premium CPG brand.

As a cultural anthropologist and student of American food culture, I quickly recognized that Caulipower and Halo Top share one fascinating thing in common that remarkably few folks seem willing to point out. They are very clever weight-management products.

What? Pizza, ice cream . . . weight management? Are you crazy? How much did I pay for this book?

Hold on. I'm not saying these brands equate to brands like Nutrisystem and Hydroxycut, which explicitly promise fairly dramatic "weight loss." Rather, these premium product lines are doing something much cleverer.

They are using:

. . . modern attributes
  . . . for the first time
    . . . in mainstream, all-American categories

---

37. The operational genius required to actually ride the unicorn is easy to underestimate. Entrepreneurs have limited access to their peers' internal workings. Trade journalists, who are continuously fed company PR language from entrepreneurs, have even less unfiltered access to what is going on inside these private companies.

. . . to connect symbolically to the second most monetizable dietary outcome in food and beverage—weight management.

So, how did I come to this grandiose conclusion?

Well, firstly, no matter what forced choice list of dietary goals are listed in a general population survey, weight management is generally near, but not quite at, the top of the list.[38] (Figure 5)

Figure 5: Weight Management as a Key Dietary Outcome

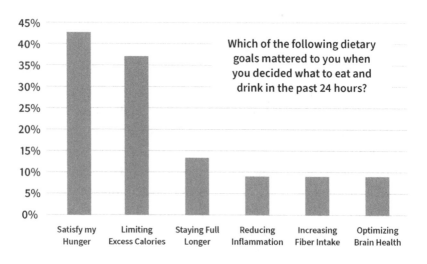

Secondly, humans have very few actual dietary needs that require deep thought to fulfill. Yet, as modern cultural actors living in affluent and complex societies, we have learned to develop ever more nuanced desired outcomes as we navigate our social lives. You may not think weight management is the product of modernity, but it really is.

Since the mid-19th century, weight management has been the most widespread, socially arbitrary dietary "need" in American society. If you doubt its relationship to affluent modern societies, spend

---

38. Premium Growth Solutions survey, 2019; n = 1,500 adults. This data corresponds to what respondents *consciously* recall thinking about; that's why the number for "satisfying my hunger" is not 100%.

some time among the poor in developing countries, as I have had. If you do, you'll encounter a widespread belief that chubbiness/obesity is a sign of wealth, power, and even sexiness. In many traditionally peasant societies, getting fat is literally a positive social ideal to this day. Only the poor and weak are thin, so this logic goes.

Only recently and among a global elite has being thin become a social ideal, primarily among elite professionals who (surprise!) also tend to drive the early growth of many premium CPG brands (and who are often their founders, too). In the United States, the elite use weight management as a tool for social distinction from the increasingly obese masses around them. The desire for superior health and longevity is now a moral requirement within this group. Obesity is a grave moral sin. This explains, in part, why categories that are intuitively about gluttony and hedonic bliss (e.g., soda) can now be viewed through a lens of ascetic restraint. In fact, diet sodas actually started this trend way back in the 1960s.

Moving forward, I have replaced the phrase *dietary need* with *dietary outcome*. Outcomes are simply desired end states for the consumer. This better connotes the level of scientific objectivity that CPG entrepreneurs should employ as they plan their own offerings and growth strategies. Consumers want outcomes. They vary in their degree of grandiosity. Your job is to deliver those outcomes. Products (and brands) are simply a means to an end, however banal it may be.

One of my favorite techniques for discovering a product line's subconsciously shared, cultural connection to the dietary outcome of weight management is to look at Google keyword search volumes over the last five years on the Google Trends platform. To do this, I generate a keyword search volume for a key symbol on the product's packaging, such as "low calorie" or "low fat" or "cauliflower." Sometimes the attribute is implied. Sometimes it is right there on the front panel. Sometimes it's the attribute you forgot to put on the front panel. When search volumes show spikes in January that fade away as the year goes on, it generally indicates that a cultural connection to a weight-management outcome is driving consumer interest in that category or in the product's key attribute. (Figure 6)

Figure 6: Googling Weight Management Symbols

"Low Calorie" Search Trends on Google – Past 5 years ending week of Oct. 20, 2019

"Cauliflower" Search Trend on Google – Past 5 years ending week of Oct. 20, 2019

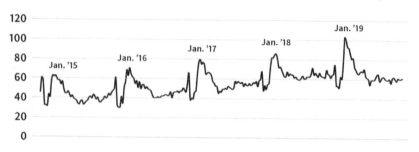

Unicorn growth is driven by culture, not founders—as indicated by these Google keyword search-volume results for terms "low-calorie" (Halo Top) and "cauliflower" (Caulipower), both of which are associated with weight-management outcomes.[39]

In the case of Caulipower, we see a classic trending weight-management structure to searches for "cauliflower," where the January spikes are growing YoY in a geometric fashion. This is the sign not of a fad but of a major bankable ingredient trend that is building over time.

Two softer reasons to believe cauliflower everything will find a permanent place in our processed food diet are:

1. It is already a commonly known, mass-market vegetable.

2. It has a stigma that lends big-market advantage to food processors: the nasty, dead-fish stench that suffocates you

---

39. Google Trends (https://www.google.com/trends). Premium Growth Solutions analysis.

when you cook it. Ugh. In an era where the open-concept kitchen is dominant, cooked cauliflower has a real problem.

What better way for America to get its old friend cauliflower back into its collective belly than to bury it in other tasty foods, like pizza crust as a low-carb starch replacement? I suspect the aural isomorphism of "flower" and "flour" isn't hurting their sales, either.

In the case of Halo Top, there is a high volume, predictable spike in interest in "low calorie" *everything* every single January. Interest very slowly tapers off as one hits December, then it spikes wildly again (our annual ritual of guilty self-reflection over holiday dietary excess, plus all those holiday photos in which we are confronted with our continued fatness).

More on Halo Top's timing success in a bit.

———————

Both of these extreme examples reveal a broader principle that goes into successful premium product design. Your product line needs to intuitively connect to dietary outcomes with high daily table stakes in everyday life. In other words, the social consequences of not achieving those outcomes should be, or at least be perceived to be, very problematic in terms of the consumer's everyday impression management in her or his social life.[40]

High-stakes dietary outcomes are generally related to conquering deep social fears and to managing our human insecurity about how others view us. Although I focus on weight management here, I've come across at least 12 other high-stakes dietary outcomes desired by very large swaths of the U.S. population.

Let's see how this kind of symbolic thinking sounds in the subconscious of certain predisposed Americans:

———————

40. The premier investigator into social impressions and how ordinary folks manage them is the late Erving Goffman, an American sociologist. Goffman authored numerous works, but most important in my view are his books *Stigma: Notes on the Management of Spoiled Identity* (1963) and *The Presentation of Self in Everyday Life* (1956).

- *If I gain lots of weight, I will worry about what others will think of me every day when I leave the house. I will also worry about my health and what others think about my health and about my ability to do my job.* These two culturally generated anxieties cover a large swath of the population, in my ethnographic research experience.[41]

- *If I don't eat satiating food, I get cranky, lightheaded, and perform poorly at work. Then, I overeat later and feel like crap about myself.*

- *If I eat something with tree nuts in it, I could go into anaphylaxis. Getting rushed to the ER is super embarrassing, especially if it's from the middle of a business meeting. That would suggest to my boss that I wasn't prepared to manage my personal issues at work.*

By the way, the above internal dialogues all derive from my ethnographic research into American food culture. I have spoken with premium CPG consumers who, when given the space and the right prompts, will unpack these kinds of arguments. They give us a sense of what a high-stakes dietary outcome looks and feels like in our subconscious mind.

Here is an outcome that is *not* high stakes: *I'm worried that I didn't optimize my trace mineral intake during the last week (in which I did skip a few meals, worked 50 hours, watched 10 hours of TV, and slept too much after drinking).* My hunch is that this person needs a therapist more than a premium supplement line. But you're welcome to chase them for a sale.

This kind of outcome is not commonly sought, because the consumer does not believe she will suffer a negative social consequence in the near term if she does not achieve the desired outcome on a daily basis. You have to be super neurotic to care deeply about something that doesn't affect your immediate social life. Not optimizing one's

---

41. Surveys are notoriously bad at assessing these kinds of latent, image-related social fears because they are deeply repressed in most cases, even though they affect consumer purchasing all the time.

trace-mineral intake over several months might result in a physical consequence—such as deficiencies in a few micronutrients, like iron or vitamin D. Unless that physical consequence disrupts one's social life, however, it just isn't high stakes to most consumers. It's possible that a doctor might convince you of a vitamin deficiency, but that would immediately make the concern a social one, not one drummed up by you on your couch, surfing the internet. Folks who do care about bleeding-edge, trace-mineral outcomes tend to hang out with each other, you'll notice, because very few people share their ideological concerns and virtually none are intrigued by them. They seem "weird" or "overdone" for a reason. If you live in certain parts of greater LA, you're around so many people like this all the time, it may be hard to see this as non-normative. Fresno's not sounding so bad now, eh?

The social stakes variable explains why so many hardcore nutritional innovations (e.g., kale chips) fail to scale. They can't find anyone beyond the alt nutrition crowd to persuade. If you ever want to meet these folks, you can find them chatting up the owner at your local supplement store. They're talking shop. Please don't interrupt. They really don't like that.

If we step back and think about the primary ways in which premium CPG excludes itself from shopper consideration, the need to appeal to large-scale dietary outcomes becomes more critical.

1. About 90 percent of shoppers in any given category don't want to pay typical price premiums for new CPG brands offering modern attributes.

2. Your brand is in limited retail outlets (or has limited online visibility) in the early years and, therefore, can't actually access all of the 10 percent of local folks in play.

These two depressing facts explain why you absolutely must ensure that your overall design connects symbolically to high-stakes outcomes for the consumer. Weird outcomes add a needless barrier to adoption.

The Law of the Attribute-Outcome Symbolism

Despite the power of connecting your brand to high-stakes dietary outcomes, it is not enough to design a package that screams an outcome like "weight management" (i.e., Nutrisystem, awkwardly) and to then go take a nap while your co-man cranks out the cases. For one thing, consumers of *new* premium offerings prefer to come to their own conclusions about which products fulfill their dietary requirements. They don't enjoy being talked down to by companies: "Let me explain to you, little consumer person, what this is good for." They want to establish for themselves whether or not your product line is a good way to meet a specific dietary outcome of interest to them. If they come to this conclusion on their own, they end up being more powerful early brand-advocates to the next tier of consumers. This is how my B2B business works, too.

So, how do ordinary folks figure out that Halo Top and Caulipower are weight-management products when they shop?

The answer to the above question rests, in part, on accepting three key assumptions of cultural anthropology:

1. Human social communities are based on shared values (despite the frequent quibbling about the details).

2. These values do not operate consciously; they operate unconsciously, on autopilot.

3. These values can only be surfaced indirectly or by peeling away layers of surface narrative to uncover the fundamental value structure at stake in specific social decisions. The decision to pick this or that CPG item is always a social decision, even when the item is picked up and consumed in total isolation. This is because consumers learn to interpret the symbols on CPG packages in a social setting, not in isolation, much like we learn any language.

Now, back to our darling unicorns!

Halo Top launched in 2012, the same year another high-protein/ low-carb ice cream brand, Wink, also launched. They both used protein isolates in their products but for very different reasons.

Wink, like its predecessor, Arctic Zero, went to market as a non-dairy ice cream (ostensibly, for vegans). The protein was used as part of a texture trick to mimic the viscosity of regular ice cream. This product design was not terribly risky. Non-dairy imitation foods have a long and stable, but ultimately small, market-share position in the premium food/beverage marketplace. (Non-dairy milks are a large exception to that rule).[42]

In contrast, Halo Top went to market as a "high protein" ice cream—which, quite frankly, still sounds wrong in so many ways. (Yet, it has now become acceptable.) "High protein ice cream" has the ring of a meat snacks/dessert mash-up no one needs a sample of ever. Culturally speaking, protein is an irrelevant and alien symbol within the language we use to describe any super-indulgent dessert category. Nuts? Yes. But protein? No one eats ice cream for a nutritional boost. The ice cream *occasion* is all about secular sin.

After its initial years of sputtering in the market, Halo Top figured out something that Wink did not: its calorie count per pint was unusually low in the category. This meant their bizarre attempt to sell a "healthy" ice cream, a cultural absurdity no marketer can just wish away, had gotten in the way of something much more powerful. That is, Halo Top offered the ultimate weight-management prize: a

---

42. Almond milk had a unique set of advantages in capturing market share that you won't find in most other plant-based, engineered, alternative food/beverage products: (1) daily consumption by heavy users, (2) high protein-to-carb ratio, bringing in lots of non-lactose–intolerant fluid milk consumers, (3) a growing number of lactose-intolerant consumers, due to the increase of Hispanics and Asians in the U.S. population, and (4) an aging population prone to developing lactose intolerance. The key variables Halo Top has that most other plant-based products don't have are daily heavy consumption and the ability to bring in millions of non-lactose-intolerant heavy users quickly.

great-tasting, "low calorie" indulgence with a minimum of synthetic trickery.[43]

Halo Top released a major packaging redesign in 2015, at the beginning of the summer ice cream season.[44] The original Halo Top package had a fairly typical case of new product feature-itis. The front panel listed "good source of protein," "all natural," "light," "7g protein," "70 calories," and "4g net carbs." In journalism, this is called *burying the lead,* and it is very common among new entrepreneurs who do not understand basic CPG front-panel design principles. Symbol-crowded front panels like this one give consumers no way to quickly form a single, powerful, attribute-outcome association. What's more, "good source of protein" unfortunately occupied the top position, where the trademark should always be. Whoops. Clutter shuts down the ability for busy shoppers to quickly scan the product's key symbols and to detect relevance to outcomes they're subconsciously seeking.

In contrast, the revised Halo Top package design all but screams "low calorie" in a category where sugar-free, "light" ice creams have never sold well. (FYI, "sugar-free" on indulgent sweet products is American cultural code for "tastes awful.")[45] The new package is also cleaner and less cluttered, allowing a busy shopper's brain to promptly grab on to the front package, memorize its key symbolism, and form a quick association with one of many weight management outcomes. The shiny golden cap doesn't hurt with memorability, either.

Halo Top used a major packaging update to make a super clear, easy-to-understand, attribute-outcome connection in the collective unconscious of a very large, predisposed consumer audience.[46] Remember what I said in the Introduction: Every 24 hours, at least

---

43. Since Halo Top did not focus on vegans to begin with, they actually had regular dairy ice cream. Their texture and flavor profile were closer to the real thing, anyway.

44. To see Halo Top's original packaging, go here: https://www.packagingstrategies.com/articles/93473-halo-top-ice-creams-unlawfully-good-product-and-packaging

45. I estimate the low-sugar, light ice cream market was roughly $50–60M in annual sales in the U.S. in the past year. AC Nielsen Scantrack, Total U.S., xAOC channels, past 52 weeks, quad week ending 5/18/2019.

46. Remember, too, that attribute-outcome signaling is a cognitive process that is *barely conscious* but is retrievable through careful, open-ended interviewing.

30 percent of American adults, on average, consciously adjust their diet to minimize calorie intake. And those are just the consumers that consciously remember doing it. This audience is much larger than the 4–5 percent of American adults today who are vegans who crave ice cream.[47]

The more educated among Halo Top's new target know that popular, at-home indulgent treats, like muffins, a handful of packaged cookies, brownies, and slices of cake or pie, each have anywhere from 400 to 600 calories—calories anchored in sugar and refined carbs. These folks already like ice cream and are actively looking for lower-calorie or calorie-equivalent alternative treats. As routine ice cream consumers will confess only in well-run, one-on-one interviews, they also often finish the whole pint in one blow. So naughty.

When a premium CPG brand can create an extremely focused and clear visual communication of symbolic attributes tied to high-stakes dietary outcomes, above-average growth is usually at hand. This requires making bold choices to banish dozens of competing symbols from your front panel. Simple front panels are hard to finalize, even at BigCo. But the most successful CPG brands in history continue to feature them. Tropicana. Oreos. Lays.

You have to make ruthless symbolic choices if you want the Law of Attribute-Outcome Symbolism to work in your brand's favor. You must eliminate the consumers' cognitive labor of sorting through package symbols. Even your predisposed consumer is shopping each category at a fast clip, even on a 45- to 60-minute shopping trip.

The human brain is exceptionally good at deleting signal noise as you navigate the environment. The *thalamus* is the portion of our brains dedicated to prioritizing signals for higher-level processing and directing them to the right places. The key finding from modern neuroscience here is that human brains are designed to *forget* most new signals—unless those signals can trigger something memorable. And memorability in social domains is context-sensitive. That's where high-stakes dietary outcomes become so critical. If your prod-

---

47. Premium Growth Solutions survey, 2019; n = 500 adults.

uct can tap into situationally-relevant social fears and promise to manage them even slightly better, your package symbolism will make it through the thalamus's fierce gatekeeping. Then, it can be seen as a relevant, known symbol worth some brain time. A symbol that is just plain weird may also make it through, but if it gets sent to the "'WTH?'" processing region, you've just weirded out the individual involved. You've spelt-ed them with your thing.

Consider both thalamic gatekeeping and the fact that a typical grocery store (including Whole Foods and Sprouts) carries 30,098 items, on average. This means a standard supermarket gondola (six-by-eight-foot shelving units that make up one side of an aisle) has anywhere from 50 to 100 different UPCs every six feet along a 100-foot aisle. (Figure 7) That means an immense amount of signal filtering is going on with your average shopper. That is also why some people leave the store tired after a big shopping trip and still managed to miss a few items that were right in front of them as they shopped.

Figure 7: Typical Supermarket Gondola

Brick and mortar shopping involves massive amounts of computing power. (Still think online grocery won't catch on eventually?)

To get through the gate of the arrogantly selective human thalamus, today's CPG entrepreneurs must create a high degree of memorability at the shelf early on.[48]

The Law of Formulation Anchoring

If you want to scale fast, you don't want to target dietary outcomes that have either low social stakes *or* ultra-low interest in the general population or, even worse, both. Instead, you need to know which high-value dietary outcomes have the broadest appeal in your category, outcomes that could plausibly connect to your product line.

This is not simply a matter of measuring conscious interest on surveys. First, I recommend collecting smart, inferential data by interacting with category consumers in real life. Time spent learning, specifically, how folks consume your products in their daily lives has another benefit. It boosts team morale far better than a trade show, PR interview, pitch slam, or anything else I can think of. It certainly beats standing in a grocery aisle and counting the tons of people walking right by your baby. Weep. Tissue.

The qualitative insights gained from actual end users will yield a rough, initial list of prioritized desired outcomes that the consumer is open to fulfilling in a specific category. Quantifying the appeal of various dietary outcomes is usually not of critical interest to founders in the early part of the Ramp. At that stage, determining the relative size of appeal is typically more than enough.

The key to obtaining relevant qualitative insights is to spend time discovering how the category is consumed on real-life consumption occasions. This is not done from your coworking office. You must take pains to locate repeat purchasing fans and to have one-on-one con-

---

48. If you want to see how good you are at ignoring inbound signals, take this selective attention test: https://www.youtube.com/watch?v=vJG698U2Mvo.

versations with them about how they use your products and why your products matter to them on specific occasions.[49]

During any consumer research on fans of your product line, you want to isolate a desired consumer outcome to which you can symbolically connect your product. Then, your goal as a business strategist is to race to own that symbolic connection in your category before someone else does. Anchoring the strategic outcome in your product's formulation is fundamental to such competitively advantaged innovation. You don't have to be unique; you just need to be competitively advantaged to drive scale.

The most common mistake founders make when going down this route is to isolate an outcome that:

1. All products in their category already serve due to category-wide formulation practices

2. And to do this without a formulation that delivers on the outcome in a more modern, powerful manner than its peers

Oops.

The latter is critical for CPG entrepreneurs to understand. You do not have the cash or other resources to turn on the huge advertising megaphones required to own a category-wide dietary outcome by screaming louder and more often than better-funded incumbents. That is a well-known BigCo tactic whose efficacy is well documented by marketing scientists. It is what enables them to be fast followers of successful premium innovations. Nice for them. You are not them.

Instead, you must have a formulation that gives you some kind of competitive lead time. You must be truly innovative at the product level. You don't necessarily have to be the first to market. You just need to be the first to dominate attention for a specific attribute-outcome connection in the consumers' minds. If you're the ninth to come out of

---

49. Some of my work involves advising founders on scrappy research techniques, but I don't sell this as a service myself. Instead, interested readers should consider taking my online course. Visit "Founder Resources" on my website for the most recent link to register. www. premiumgrowthsolutions.com

the gate but the first to break out and ride the Skate Ramp, no one will care that eight others launched before you. You'll still be the leader.

Let's look at some examples of attribute-outcome signals that are and are not anchored in the formulations of a specific product line.

- **Kombucha.** Most consumers see kombucha as a "healthy" category, which is how it entered American popular culture in the 1990s. Talking generically about how your kombucha brand is healthier than soda/energy drinks because of its probiotics or because it's more natural than conventional diet drinks does not create maximal competitive advantage, because *any* kombucha brand gets credit for being natural and probiotic-rich.

  If you want to be a healthier kombucha brand that commands a premium (above private label, in this case), you could have a super-high probiotic count or something else to serve as symbolic validation of your claim to being the "healthiest" kombucha. That could get you outsized attention, if connected to the right dietary outcome and promoted properly. Vague attributes like "healthy" not tied to a brand-specific formulation generate weak memorability and even weaker competitive advantage. You can still grow, but you'll have to rely more heavily on tons of paid advertising of the trademark itself to generate memorability. Not great, unless you're rich. Guessing you're not.

- **Cottage cheese.** Cottage cheese has always been a "low-fat" snack to which dieters have gravitated. Cottage cheese is also inherently "high in protein," just the way it has always been made. Yet, no one really marketed a product line around that notion until recently (Good Culture, in 2015). Can a brand shift the conversation from "low-fat" weight management to "protein-rich" weight management? Potentially.

However, that is a risky approach for a product line whose formulation cannot be anchored strongly to that attribute-outcome signal without significant funding to turn on the megaphone. Even then, incumbent big dairy companies can easily and quickly re-do their packaging or up their protein content and put a cap on your growth. Again, significant funding would be necessary to drive communications amplitude and own a specific protein-outcome signal in the category.

If, for the sake of continuity, we return to the Halo Top case, we can learn a best practice the company did through a similar immersion with consumers. As discussed earlier in this chapter, Halo Top connected with the consumers' weight-management outcome by distinguishing itself as a "low-calorie" ice cream brand. Those who know the ice cream category are aware that the most horrifying experience of category fans is to realize they've just finished the entire pint and thereby blown their diet for the day and flooded their bloodstream with sugar. While this self-sabotaging behavior is not especially common, the desire to avoid it is disproportionately great. In other words, the social stakes of not sabotaging one's weight-management goals (which are always social) are so high for a specific section of the population that they are prone to exaggerating their dietary risks.

The real strategic prize is found when your product line takes a culturally popular outcome (often associated with other categories) and suddenly unleashes it in a category where no one has offered it before. This is what Chobani did, more or less accidentally, with Greek yogurt by distributing it in mainstream supermarket channels in New York and Pennsylvania. In those states, consumers most likely had very little interest in Chobani's "ethnic" origin and more interest in the protein-satiety connection it unleashed in a tired, processed category in which "organic purity" had been the primary premium strategy up until then.

In addition, Chobani had the advantage of Greek yogurt's well-known sensory effect on the human stomach. Consumers tend to feel much fuller after a cup of Greek than after a cup of ordinary low-fat or fat-free yogurt. Whenever there is a sensory experience that corroborates (or lends meaning to) a product line's attribute-out-come symbolism, the innovation is particularly advantaged for rapid growth—including unicorn growth. It's the trifecta of CPG innovation.

One of the most common mistakes CPG founders continue to make is to confuse their own personal drivers for founding their company with the category-relevant demand drivers that will provide maximal acceleration and long-term scalability. This is most prevalent in mission-driven brands, where the mission is actively projected onto the business as the main reason to scale the brand and where attention to detail on the product-design side can be quite weak.

The root cause of this confusion is less likely the individual founder's self-involvement than it is their unwitting disrespect for the consumer who will eventually build their brand. Founders who do not do their category homework tend to be ones who see the consumer as a passive, even fawning, recipient of their innovation—not as the engine of their eventual success and not as an implicit business partner. Based on years of experience deconstructing what drove the fast ramping of premium CPG brands, I can tell you this: You are serving consumers. Not the other way around. Forget this at your own peril.

The growth of founder worship in the trade media, podcasts, etc. is a disturbing cultural trend that only runs counter to the actual humility required to finalize and ramp a winning product. The founders whose product lines grow fast become category experts in a professional sense (via competitive and consumer insights) as quickly as possible, and they plan their strategies accordingly. The time to study your category this deeply is in the first $500,000, not when you're at $10 million.

The Power of Focus, or the Law of Frito-Lay

There is another critical law of product design that, ironically, even BigCo has frequently overlooked in their obsession with lower-risk, line-extension innovation: the Power of Focus. This law is not specific to premium CPG brands. In fact, SC Johnson is perhaps the single most consistent adherent to it within CPG. But this book features food/beverage case studies, so I'm calling it the *Law of Frito-Lay*. Besides, Cheetos are a lot more fun than Scrubbing Bubbles. Sorry. It's just true.

I've had the pleasure of consulting with Frito-Lay North America several times in my career. Of all the BigCo clients in my roster, FLNA continues to be the most consistently world-class marketer in CPG. They have one of the largest distribution capabilities in the world, allowing them to reach over 290,000 retail outlets within weeks of a launch.[50] For context, there are 38,000 supermarket doors in the United States (including Walmart), and Frito-Lay is in every one of them. Despite its God-like ability to shove product in front of consumers, FLNA focuses just as hard on building memorability as it does on building distribution with their core trademarks. Heard of the Superbowl? A decent cultural argument can be made that the Superbowl is more a field marketing event for PepsiCo (Frito-Lay's parent company) than it is the NFL season finale. If Frito-Lay could get each team to wear Doritos co-branded Superbowl jerseys, they would, trust me.

FLNA has eight entirely distinct salty snack forms, each of which has a uniquely iconic sensory experience for which it has basically no competition at all. Private-label knockoffs sell relatively pitiful amounts of even the best-executed imitations (which you'll find at ALDI, in my experience). Mere distribution cannot explain the creation of so many, nearly-identical salty-snack products with nine- and ten-figure revenue. World-class R&D coupled with unrelenting focus on a single product form with multiple flavors is a proven value-added CPG brand-building strategy.

One form. One sensory experience. One trademark. It works so well because it's simple. *Simplicity facilitates maximum memorability in*

50. Frito-Lay Fact Sheet: www-frito-lay.com

the consumer's mind. The only serious variation the brain has to grasp is surface flavor. The rest of the brand is essentially repetition and ruthless consistency. Rinse. Repeat.

I continue to see a bewildering number of premium CPG brands trying to obtain topline growth through premature platforming. Platforming is the practice of spreading your trademark across multiple unrelated categories, sometimes multiple aisles. In the near term, it can often lift total revenue because it simply accesses more eyeballs merely by increasing the amount of UPCs any given shopper sees. However, prior research by The Hartman Group has already established that single-category, early-stage premium food/beverage brands outperform multi-category ones as they scale toward $100 million because they are far more likely to sustain high growth rates.[51] (Figure 8) Their multiple-category equivalents tend, statistically, to see their growth rates collapse as they scale—which neither a founder nor a strategic acquirer want.

Figure 8: Single-Category Brands Outperform Multi-Category Ones

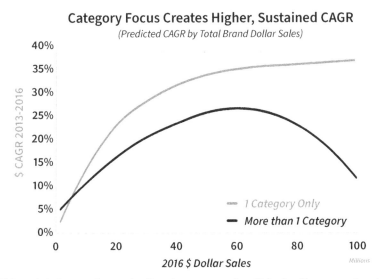

This analysis draws on thousands of brands across more than 25 food and beverage categories.

---

51. AC Nielsen Scantrack, Total U.S., xAOC channels, past four years, quad week ending 12/31/2016. Analysis courtesy of The Hartman Group, Inc.

CHAPTER 4

DISCOVERING YOUR
KEY ATTRIBUTES

One reason weight management is such a mass-appeal consumer outcome is that modern American life constantly messes with our ability to achieve even the most diluted standard we set for it. Our increasingly on-demand work schedules can also lead to meal skipping and even snack forgetting. The uneven availability of "real food" options outside the home leads to choices we later regret. Then there are our many, many cravings for all things salty, sweet, and carb-heavy.

But something much more specific to the premium CPG marketplace is driving phenomenal growth in weight management and other highly desired dietary outcomes: the spread of increasingly more difficult to attain health, fitness, and body-image goals.

Goals like:

- Low body fat percentage, regardless of age (WTH?)

- Low blood pressure and low resting heart rate, like a triathlete in his or her prime

- Bodybuilder levels of strength, idolized in action movies and fitness subcultures (i.e., Marvel, CrossFit, the shredded old guy at the gym who embarrasses us all)

- Idealized blood sugar and blood cholesterol metrics (again, the triathlete paradigm of fitness, which is totally inconsistent with the Wal-merican diet)

These and other extreme health standards have led to a very large relative disparity between where the average adult perceives themselves to be and where they aspire to be. The norm of a successful adult has been redefined to include "fit." So, our diets have become highly moralized as a result. When people are called out for dietary moralizing (i.e., "stop talking like a self-righteous little prima donna"), they usually cover with some pragmatic euphemism about seeking "longevity" or "quality of life." Really? Hmmm. It's really about three to five extra years when you're 85 or 90? You really look at your existence like a return-on-principal calculation? You might want to join the trace-mineral optimizers in therapy.

Medical authorities don't argue for anything nearly as stringent as the health ideals that popular media culture spreads to a large number of people. That's the power of collectively shared values. In this case, what once emerged from the urban margins of American life—e.g., CrossFit gyms, triathlons, bodybuilding gyms, Venice Beach, fitness chefs—is now coming at us straight from our mobile screens in the form of the Marvel superhero body aesthetic. Kinobody is a new training brand that has taken inspiration from Marvel superhero mania and turned it into a monetizable fitness program. Everything but the vibranium Captain America shield.

In short, our modern urban diet has become hyper-moralized to a standard that few will ever attain, yet millions attempt to attain. It is the second great moral revolution in American food culture, after the one related to broader weight management that began in the

1950s. It's also different from, but compatible with, natural processing standards.[52]

I'm not even quite sure, yet, what to call this cluster of emerging
outcomes. But I know "health and wellness" is not the right phrase.
Wal-merican BigCo executives use empty phrases like "health and
wellness"; smart CPG innovators do not.

What this particular area of urban food culture reveals is the ability for non-food cultural domains and ideals to push us to utilize ever
more creative and supposedly scientific formulations and magical ingredients to achieve these modern outcomes.

Of course, other cultural forces are also reshaping modern, urban food culture. In this book I focus on those related to new notions
of hyper-moralized health because they've created nine-figure businesses the most reliably and the most quickly. Just think about how
much consumers have been worrying about their daily protein intake
over the past 15 years, when they didn't give it a thought in the 1990s.
That's culture at work, folks. Insidious. God-like. Socially construct-
ed. Difficult to completely resist.

Emerging brands have and will continue to play a role in driving new attributes, such as protein intake, from obscurity (or irrele-
vance) into the heart of our everyday dietary concerns. Healthy eating
trends, in general, provide very reliable cultural tailwinds for those
CPG founders who want to ramp their brand, because consumers easily give an ear to the next best thing. And they always will, because the
ideals they're chasing are largely impossible to attain to begin with.
They are religious in nature.

Many premium Skate Ramp brands have learned, sometimes
by accident, that the secret to exponential growth is to *reframe* how

---

52. I recognize that allergen avoidance is often brought up as a purchase driver for natural
foods that does not appear to fit the sociological model I'm describing here. However, when
you look into the percentage of allergen avoiders who actually have a confirmed medical allergy
diagnosis, you will discover that most of the allergy-avoiding behavior is actually an adjunct to
modern notions of purity. It is also often strongly linked to aspirations of elite social status,
where a hyper-individualized diet is becoming normative (despite how much it conflicts with
collective rituals like the family dinner).

consumers should seek an established dietary outcome of high cultural value and high social stakes for the individual consumer. (See Chapter 3.)

I don't use the word reframe loosely. The key is to isolate modern attributes that reframe what healthy means in a specific operating category or that introduce "healthy" to a category for the first time. This task requires some guardrails; otherwise, founders can easily wander into the tarpit of the weird as f*^k.

Selecting a modern dietary attribute involves the careful use of existing, but not mass-market, cultural symbolism and category context in a way that triggers powerful attribute/outcome associations in the consumer's mind. Selecting an unfamiliar context (e.g., ice cream or pizza) is also key to generating maximum memorability—as well as to getting past the busy shopper's thalamus.

Don't try to use obscure symbolism to pull this off. I'm talking about the tendency of CPG entrepreneurs doing the "healthy innovation" thing to innovate deep inside the murky fog of cultural obscurity. Yes, tempeh is still obscure, 50 years after its market introduction— and for good reason! You can have your spelt-grain, tempeh, and raw sprouts sandwich with vegan mayonnaise. Enjoy it without me. I hope you learn to love yourself someday.

Obscure attributes don't easily connect with established, broad dietary outcomes without significant consumer education and the passage of time. Either factor fights against rapid acceleration and growth. If time is not critical to your plan, then, by all means, that's a valid zone for long-term innovation. Many early premium brands, like Stonyfield yogurt and Essentia water, walked this slow pace from their inception and eventually scaled, though not at a pace most founders and any investors today would want to experience.

Most founders want to find *advantaged* attributes to help reframe "healthy" at the category level.

Advantaged attributes that unlock growth quickly are generally:

- Tied to a new "natural" formulation requiring some proprietary R&D. (Otherwise, incumbents will outflank you on the shelf in a fast-following marketing blitz.)

- New in the category to date (e.g., high-protein yogurt in 2005)

- Connectable to established high-stakes dietary outcomes (e.g., weight management) or rapidly scaling ones (e.g., digestive comfort)

- Based on a hard-to-replicate formulation (e.g., Spindrift's simple avoidance of flavoring additives), which will give you time to scale before followers can figure it out

- Already helped another premium CPG brand scale in another category

But are *not*:

- Currently obscure in all categories (e.g., SAM-e, noni berry, teff, aroniaberries, tempeh). Just because an ingredient is well known among industry insiders due to faddish media coverage doesn't mean it has escaped obscurity with the larger population required to scale a brand.

- Currently obscure and undiscussed in the popular culture of the urban elite. (In other words, key influencers should have been talking about it for three to five years already.)

- Connotatively risky (for example, "raw" or "spent")

- Tied to closed, cultish, and/or militant consumer niches—lifestyle groups so extreme in their eating code they alienate almost everyone and fail to inspire/persuade outsiders easily (e.g., vegans, the hyper-allergic, severe auto-immune syndrome sufferers, chemical sensitivity sufferers, people with celiac disease, etc.)

- Suggestive of unpleasurable/unknown sensory qualities (e.g., spelt grain, gluten-free, inscrutable flavor/varietal names that draw a total and utter blank)

Phew.

If the key attribute is new to the category (which it often is in good premium CPG innovations), there is one final watch-out. To explain it, though, I need to refer back to those interminable, cherry-picked, recycled trend lists that you should stop reading immediately. If mushroom tea makes one of those lists three years in a row, you might reasonably ask yourself: *Is mushroom now an attribute with which I can reframe a category? Should I raise some money and launch a mushroom soda, or a mycoprotein sports drink, or a mycoprotein bar? What if I don't act now? Will I be too late on the mushroom everything trend?* (Cue: gnashing of teeth, wringing of hands, biting of nails.)

The baseline is, your attribute/category combination must at least trigger an immediately neutral response in the consumer's mind. That is all that's really required—essentially, a subconscious *huh*. This neutral reaction signifies that the listener is able to imagine the key attribute not being in conflict with normal sensory and/or cultural expectations in the category. The rest of the formula to unleash a modern attribute is honestly part grit and part persistence and knowing where in urban retail (and foodservice) to show up, based on how large the addressable market is right now for your attribute-outcome combination.

What you *don't* want is an immediate reaction of disgust and incredulity from the majority of urban, educated listeners. That signifies your magical attribute has crossed an implicit cultural boundary of sensory acceptability. Such rules are anchored in deeply held food traditions. And you don't want to fight those, even if your formulation is amazing in the mouth. That would place an enormous word-of-mouth marketing burden on your young brand, much like using an obscure attribute that requires education. Why, again, do I care about aroniaberries? Ooh, because I need to maximize my antioxidant intake on a daily basis? Really?

Back to mushrooms. Have you noticed that most of the products on these industry trend lists are just . . . well . . . really weird? Are you afraid to say this for fear of being a killjoy who doesn't get it? Do you wonder if you're the only one who thinks half the stuff is weird, gross, just plain off?

You're not insane. Trust me. In food culture, "rare" has two possible symbolic valences: weird/obscure (e.g., eel, tempeh, vitamin K-rich) or elite (e.g., sushi rice, lemongrass, "craft" anything). The latter most of you have heard about, read about, tasted, and admire. Elite attributes that work are simply *not* Wal-merican ones. Of course, they do not have to surprise your foodie friends. Only weird sh#t would surprise them. But, as if on cue, they'll pretend they've known about it for years (as they search madly online in private for basic info about it).

If you want exponential growth soon, weird is pretty much a non-starter. When your brain says *weird*, it's tapping into a primordial omnivore aversion to bitter-tasting food that could be poisonous or indigestible.[53] Yes, humans can eat lawn grass if they want to, but the results in your GI tract won't be pleasant. You know you don't need to try this to find out whether I'm right. Your brain has many layers of signaling telling you that your gut is not evolved to handle grass like a cow (with its four-chamber super stomach). You can thank evolution. Or God. Or both.

Elite/luxury, on the other hand, is largely a pricing problem that can be solved through strategically targeting the business to just the right people, who won't care about the cost. It can also become approachable once it sells beyond the original, elite early consumers (whether single-track mountain bikers with their Clif bars or sushi geeks in 1990s San Francisco). As volume grows and the product enters normal channels of distribution, the price will come down. If it really takes, it becomes a Wal-merican "mainstay."

---

53. Anne Fischer, Yoav Gilad, Orna Man, and Svate Pääbo. "Evolution of bitter taste receptors in humans and apes." *Molecular Biology and Evolution* 22(3), (2004): 432–436.

Consumers of elite/luxury attributes are even more willing to pay a premium in specific categories that they value as critical tools in their regular dietary regimen. But the elite attribute has to be a *modern* one (e.g., fermented, keto, slow carb) and not a tired, zombie luxury attribute from a bygone era (e.g., pimento cheese, Dom Perignon, caviar).

––––––––––

If you're willing to be more patient, there is another way to think about a key attribute for premium product design that is potentially smarter for the average, undercapitalized entrepreneur discussed at the start of this book. If what I'm about to suggest aligns with your existing product line, awesome. If not, it's just an option.

That approach is to design a product that asks for a specific sensory trade-off that has symbolic value as a "wise, righteous alternative" among urban, healthy-lifestyle, food-culture influencers.

For instance, trading off sweetness for a healthier option is one of the most powerful growth engines across multiple CPG categories. It is easier to accomplish in some categories (e.g., yogurt) than in others (e.g., iconic condiments). But it is powerful.

Let's look at a real-life case of a Skate Ramp brand that successfully traded-off a sweet sensory experience for a smart symbolic experience.

Siggi's is my favorite example of leveraging this competitive advantage to essentially frighten away competitors, especially serial entrepreneurs and BigCo who tend to want an innovation they can scale in three to five years. Siggi's, if you're unfamiliar, introduced America to *skyr* (Icelandic yogurt), a product line with extremely low natural sugars and no artificial sweeteners. The über tart and über low-sugar brand took a while to catch on with urban dietary influencers, but then it ramped exponentially fast. (Figure 9)

Figure 9: Siggi's Ride Up the Skate Ramp

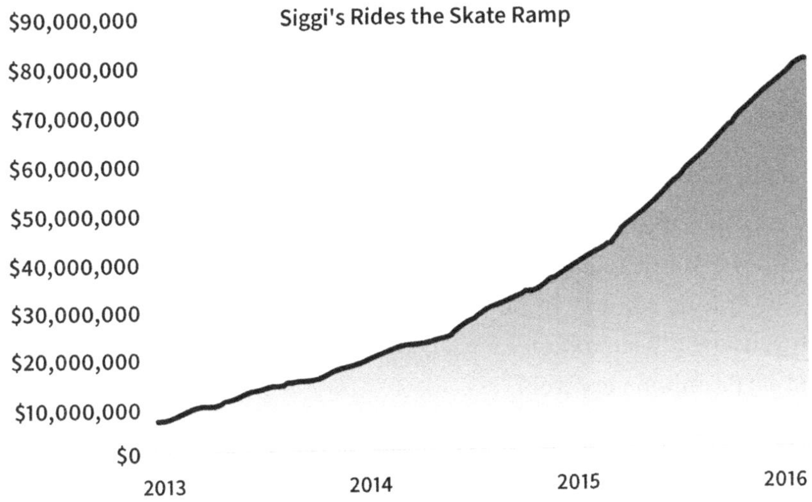

Siggi's spent seven years getting to $10 million. Then, it rapidly ramped toward $100 million, as urban food culture had finally dialed up the volume on hidden sugars in food.[54]

If you are the first premium player to do something like siggi's did in a category where mainstream market leaders (including premium brands) are sweet to very sweet, you will *not* have a lot of competition. Most would-be challengers will think you're crazy. Great. Let them. That is what you want.

Low sweetness is one of those uncommon sensory trade-offs to which your tongue and brain *can* adapt over time. If you've ever lived abroad in Asia for more than a month, you probably experienced a paralyzing phase of mind-numbing sugar cravings. When I went through it during the mid-1990s in India, it was like coming off nicotine or caffeine. Bad news. I used to run out of my apartment to the nearby bus stand and pound crappy sheet cake slices from a not-so-fancy bakery (much to the amusement of the owner and his friends). After six months of this, though, it suddenly stopped. Then, I was fine with

54. Euromonitor, 2017. Analysis courtesy of The Hartman Group, Inc.

eating a diet with extremely low sugar—no refined sugar and very few natural plant sugars.

I thought I was a freak, until years later when I saw how consumers reacted over time to siggi's. What began as a grimacing spoon-by-spoon adventure with lots of added sweeteners, slowly became, for some, adaptation to the inherent but objectively low sweetness of skyr. Once that transition is made, the consumer feels like a badass. Can you handle the sour? Can you? The sensory trade-off easily becomes a status badge in the urban de-sugaring of the American diet. This kind of sensory trade-off reduces the volume of repeat in return for insane repeat volumes among those who remain. It also sustains a price premium very well.

This approach to commanding a premium requires a lot of patience. You have to be in it for the long haul. You have to want to be first in your category to scale it. And you need to be able to avoid traditional VC involvement, for the most part. This is the only way I've ever seen being "weird" as a CPG innovator really pay off.

PART TWO

MANAGING A SMALL

EXPERIMENT

PHASE 1 $0—$1M

CHAPTER 5

CREATE A WELL-MARKED PRODUCT LINE

D esigning and launching a premium CPG product line has a couple
eerie things in common with writing and publishing a book:

- 97 percent of people who attempt to write a book lose interest and never finish.
- 3 percent finish but then realize they need to revise or start over.

And a finished manuscript that doesn't get published, bought, and read is just a paperweight, including mine.[55]

Because it can take a long time to develop a premium CPG product, I've seen many founders chase artificial timelines to scale. They're tired and need income. Often, they anchor their launch to the day they began product development rather than the day they ship their first case to a store or a distributor. I often see this reflected in the founding dates cited on LinkedIn profiles. This makes them even more hasty.

---

55. https://thesynergyexpert.com/2015/10/20/the-top-reason-people-never-finish-writing-their-book/

The day you ship your first case is the real Day 1 of your business.

It is also Day 1 of what should be considered a rolling experiment. I strongly advise founders to plan on this rolling experiment lasting two to four years, if not longer, on the way up to $1 million or more in trailing, annualized sales. If things work out really well, it can be faster. That would be great. Just don't plan on it and set yourself up for disappointment.

The more entrepreneurs overthink and thereby subconsciously overcommit to every launch detail (flavor, packaging, messaging, brand essence, etc.) *before* they have even one paid consumer, the more difficult it will be when the market responds with a loud, resounding *meh!* As Peter Rahal's father told him upon realizing his son, the founder of RXBAR, was planning a big, premature, pre-revenue fund raise, as if he had it all figured out, "You guys need to shut the fuck up and just sell a thousand bars."[56] Ouch, Mr. Rahal. As they later found out, their original pack design did not connect with the broader market. I bet he's glad he listened to Dad.

The goal of launching an experiment is to build the spirit of optimization into your company right from the start, rather than sprinting for years and waiting for a big problem to motivate you to optimize. I get plenty of calls from folks whose velocities have stalled or started to decline after they rush to seven figures without a lot of honest self-critique along the way.

So, how do you design a small-scale, undercapitalized CPG experiment in a way that increases your odds of staying on the Skate Ramp?

Learning to Ride the Ramp in Three Steps

Smart CPG founders utilize the following three steps to ensure they have something that will ride the Skate Ramp and stay on it when they

---

56. https://www.entrepreneur.com/article/308136

do hit the gas later. This is the CPG equivalent of learning basic skateboard skills on shallow, linear ramps at your local skate park *before* you boastfully attack a quarter-pipe ramp that is taller than you. You don't want to be the kid who slides back down and falls on his ass.

Here are the steps I recommend:

1. Create

   › A product line designed to command a premium *now* (see Part 1)

   › A smart trademark for your product line

2. Test

   › For initial proof of concept using early-stage key performance indicators (KPIs)

   › To discover *why* you're growing or not growing

3. Iterate

   › With a Big Mallet somewhere among the 4Ps

   › Based on understanding the 4P pyramid of causality (product, placement, price, promotion) and your competitive reality

When you first launch your CPG business, you have created the product itself, some UPCs, a package design, a package structure, and a trademark. But you have *not* created a brand. A brand is what happens to a trademark when the underlying business scales well. Brands get built off of consumer outcomes that are consistently experienced. Over time, these socially shared experiences with identical products reflect back onto the trademark, creating what is culturally referred to as a *brand*. Brand is the cultural prize you earn, not a lever you pull when you launch a new trademark into the world.[57] A great name or front-panel design is not a brand.

---

57. This is something that many large agencies serving the CPG sector still don't understand

Don't just take my word for it. To quote one of the few agency heads I know who understands this phenomenon, Ted Wright, of the WOMM agency, Fizz: "A brand = a product's qualities + consumers' conversations about said qualities + passage of time."

You can hire agencies, buy distribution, discount your product, and jump and scream at demo tables, but, ultimately, the consumer is the force that will turn your product's trademark into a brand over time. You can either embrace this reality and work with it, or ignore it at great expense (literally). I see both approaches all the time.

Successful CPG entrepreneurs don't get caught up in brand navel-gazing, in premature brand architecture, or in similar brand-overthink common at BigCo. They accept that many details of the product experience might change. This is what experimenting entails. Ironically, the one aspect of your product you *do* want to nail up front and *never* change is the one many folks confuse with brand: your master trademark.

Optimal Trademark Design

If you change your trademark after launching, you will encounter a big set of problems relating to my previous area of specialization in social science: impression management. Within the CPG industry, it is imperative that you carefully manage both your trade impressions and your investor impressions from the very beginning.

Let's look at the scenario of changing your trademark to see how this all works.

> **Trade Impressions:** From the day you start shipping cases with a new trademark, distributors and retailers will treat your business as a completely new product line. This will require a new set of UPCs, and in many cases, the reassignment of slots in distributor and retailer warehouses. If you ignore this reality and start shipping your cases of product

or have institutionally forgotten because old, established brands drive their books and their profits.

with Trademark 2.0, you *will* get caught and you *will* lose distribution slots. If that happens, you *will* go out of stock and quickly lose retail accounts as you experience extended out-of-stocks. Basically, the business could come to a swift end if you don't manage the transition very carefully. Then, you will be relaunching in front of the trade with egg on your face. All of this will undermine any attempt at aggressive negotiation with said retail buyers, who tend to remember big screw-ups for a long-time. I just watched a food brand mess this up recently, with investors on board. The brand has now wound down and sold off the trademark to partially pay down debt. A disastrous retail prom date.

Investor Impressions: You may very well bootstrap your early years if you have healthy gross margins. But most Skate Ramp brands raise some kind of money in multiple angel rounds. If you do a sloppy trademark flip, it will be discussed and remembered in a small pool of CPG investors, who talk to each other a lot (and to me). For folks who get hundreds of pitch decks a year, this is an easy reason to delete yours from their inbox. "Guy just isn't professional. . . ."

To ensure that new founders avoid experimenting with a trademark and then finding they have to switch it, I will now share some critical trademark design principles. These trademarking guardrails come out of my work studying Skate Ramp brands and iconic CPG brands in snacks and beverages.

This is where BigCo brands are actually extremely helpful mentors to new CPG brands. BigCo's stable of old trademarks tend to be highly memorable for specific linguistic reasons. They're super simple. And simple lends itself to rapid memorization and, consequently, to faster recall and to greater overall memorability of your product line.

Trademarking well actually benefits from creative underthink, unlike your package design, formulation, strategic plan, etc.

Trademark Legal Assistance

Founders still deciding on their trademark should devour the content of the United States Patent/Trademark Office (USPTO), so they can also learn the legal guardrails involved. Of course, I always recommend consulting a trademark attorney with CPG specialization to sign off on your mark's long-term defensibility. In addition, I encourage founders to study the work of David Placek's firm, Lexicon Branding, because there is an advanced level to naming, built on modern linguistics.

Trademarking Basics

Four fundamental rules facilitate low-error, first-time aural and oral recognition of your trademark. These trademarking must-dos also substantially increase the likelihood of subsequent recognition among consumers who read about your products before seeing it or hearing about it.

1. **One or two words, max.** To use a food analogy, a powerful trademark is a one-bite phenomenon. I often encounter small CPG brands that use entire phrases as their trademark. These are really taglines (and usually inferior ones) masquerading as master trademarks. Keep it super short.

2. **One to three syllables, max.** Short and snappy is far more memorable than polysyllabic and erudite. This is true in conversation as well. After leaving academia, I spent years retiring hundreds of $64,000 words that made people groan every time I used them. Don't put long, highbrow words (including arcane ingredient names) in your trademark to sound impressive. Spare us all.

3. **Easily pronounceable.** If early consumers are pronouncing your trademark multiple ways, it can hinder, rather

than foster, word-of-mouth recommendation and in-aisle recognition. Luckily, many consumers will actually memorize your pack design first, so your trademark's nebulous pronunciation may not affect repeat from those who discover you in-store first. But why create easily avoided barriers to memorability?

4. **Easy to spell,** with easy-to-hear *phonemes* (letter sounds). Many folks stink at spelling, in large part because public education in the United States has more or less abandoned phonics. Contributing to the country's dismal spelling ability is that 10 percent of the population is dyslexic, a neurological condition that, among other things, makes it difficult to translate polysyllabic words they've heard into words they can read and write. Make it easy for folks to sound out the letters of words they see on the top of your package, so they can actually read and remember them.

Premium CPG Trademarking No-Nos

A few newbie trademarking errors are very common in the premium end of CPG. Making these mistakes will artificially wound your initial experiment in the market. Although they may not be death knells, they definitely won't help your cause.

No premium CPG trademark should include:

- **Negative language**—any explicitly negative words (e.g., no, not, never) or negative prefixes (e.g., anti-, de-, non-, un-). I think this is self-explanatory, but a fundamental law of CPG strategy is that you have to stand *for* something, even if you're implicitly rebelling against something else. If your trademark is literally a complaint, however short, it will reflexively turn off many folks. This is especially true if the beverage or snack will be carried around in public, eaten in the office, or otherwise socially displayed. Keep your natural-industry crankiness to yourself. Not helpful.

- **Ingredient names.** This rule is commonly broken by idealistic premium innovators in CPG, especially by those building a custom supply chain around a new-to-market, magical ingredient. But the rule stands in my book.

  Ingredients are one of the biggest sources of product fads in CPG. It is extremely hard to predict which ones will actually transform into long-term market trends, because ingredient/outcome associations are too new culturally and often competing with one another among urban consumers. If you're an early innovator of a nutrient-dense ingredient du jour, any negative sensory associations will not have arisen yet in the broader society. Then, if a stigma does form, you will get spelt-ed when you least expect it. If you've ever had spelt-grain bread, you know what I mean. It's a cultural abomination of biblical proportions. If your key ingredient has any other forms of cultural stigma (i.e., crickets, monkey poo coffee, cockroaches, bright-colored shrooms, etc.), you've shot yourself in the foot right from the start.

  It is also critical that your trademark stands for something much bigger than its formula, down the line. Ingredients lack poetic power. They can never become iconic symbols. They drag your trademark into a tarpit of *denotations* (literal meanings) that fight the rapid development of positive *connotations* (suggested meanings) emerging from consumer experience. The latter is what turns your trademark into a brand over time. You want this process of accumulated meaning to be smooth and organic.

- **Occasions, seasons, or dayparts**—specific holidays, celebrations, or milestones (e.g., Christmas, birthday, wedding); seasonal references (e.g., winter, summer, warm weather, rainy); or designated times of day (e.g., morning, night, breakfast, lunch, dinner, daily). This kind of trademarking is not widespread, but it can be tempting. The problem is, it ties your product line to a specific moment in the consumer's mind. This is not the kind of memorability you want because it *will* work. Shoppers absolutely do shop for occasion-specific products, all the time. But they will also shop for those same products, even if they haven't been subliminally programmed to buy them specifically and solely for those occasions.

So, don't box yourself in symbolically. CPG businesses generally grow by adding relevant usage occasions as they scale. This is a major accelerant you don't want to smother early on by limiting the consumer's view of your products' relevance in their daily diet.

- **Self-righteous phrases.** This is quite common in premium CPG trademarking, so I have to put it out there. The problem with trademarks like "The Better Bar" or "Save Our Earth" is not the founder's intent, per se. It's that moralistic trademarks invite immediate opposition from haters and doubters. That's how moral argument works in human culture. Perhaps such trademarks could garner some short-term PR, but the long-term effect is that your trademark becomes less viral if consumers have to cross-check their friends and family for ideological openness before talking it up. Besides, increasingly in premium CPG, these kinds of trademarks are just plain dull.

  If you want your trademark to cleverly reflect your mission, follow the Seventh Generation model. Seventh Generation is a great trademark because the phrase has no real meaning to the uninitiated consumer, but it's mysterious enough to make the fan look into the brand's story. Then, they can learn the trademark's meaning and its relationship to the mission of the company.

Trademarking Pro Tip: Opt for the Meaningless

Yes, I have read Nietzsche, but that's not why I'm proposing that your trademark have little to no powerful meaning. Meaningless trademarks work super well because they:

- Carry no connotations or denotations that distract consumers or accidentally polarize them

- Keep your personal passions out and form a neutral meeting place between you, the product line, and the consumers who buy it

- Don't distract consumers from absorbing high-priority, attribute-outcome symbolic associations via your front panel

- Are empty linguistic vessels that fill with the meanings generated by the consumers' lived experiences when consuming your product. They will subconsciously attribute meanings and emotions to your trademark over time. When properly gathered, these meanings and associated emotions will become the raw material for early marketing pushes.

Oreo. Lay's. Chobani. Clif. Skuta. Seventh Generation. Spindrift. Annie's. Stacy's. Sabra.

Personal names (Annie's), foreign language words (Chobani), historically obscure technical words (Spindrift), and polylinguistic mash-ups (Skuta) are optimal genres of meaningless trademarks. As long as they don't connect to current celebrities, solitary personal names are curiously meaningless to most of us and yet suggest the intimacy and authenticity that consumers want from premium CPG brands.

While many details of your product offering should be an open experiment in the early years, your trademark should be one of the few fixed elements. If it isn't, not only will you be relaunching your business (more or less) and managing stigma with the trade and investors; you'll be confusing consumers, as well.

Once you've thoughtfully created a product that commands a premium in a competitively advantaged manner *and* created a killer, simple, and (hopefully) meaningless trademark, it's time to set up your in-market experiment and run some tests.

CHAPTER 6

MANAGING A SMALL EXPERIMENT

R iding the Skate Ramp is all about winning on the back half of the curve. This is counter-intuitive to BigCo launch models—which I believe is part of the reason many retail buyers still don't understand the Ramp. In the world of LittleCo, retail buyers recognize (1) face-planting by unprepared amateurs, (2) shallow geometric growth (which afflicts the majority of early-stage brands), and (3) unicorn growth, because the latter is just slightly slower than typical BigCo national launches. Buyers can see your velocities are strong, yes, but you're still just...too...damn...small...to move their profit needle. They also generally lack the long-term thinking to imagine where an exponential curve could lead in terms of future, absolute profit dollars.

In the early months and years of your experiment, you will be located in what I call *Phase 1 of the Ramp:* $0–$1 million in POS sales. (Figure 10)

Figure 10: The Skate Ramp and Its Key Revenue Phases

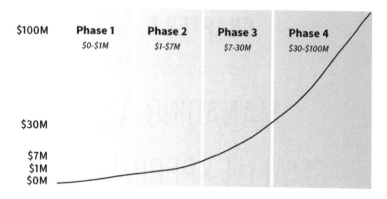

Most premium brands fail during Phase 1, somewhere on the way to $1 million in POS sales. During Phase 2, the initial momentum to $7 million enhances the ability to attract investment capital. Revenues ascend steeply toward $30 million during Phase 3, the proving grounds. Revenues rise even more steeply toward $100 million during Phase 4, when the verdict will be delivered.[58]

Although this is the tough, deleveraged reality of selling into brick-and-mortar as a small business, how you manage your journey on the lower portion of the Skate Ramp curve is where the real strategic brilliance needs to happen. These are the years when you want to:

- Get your operations right.
- Understand your business model.
- Understand your fans.
- Understand why your business is growing (or not).
- Iterate and refine your playbook at small scale.

Or . . . you may get super lucky like Caulipower, SkinnyPop, or Chobani. In those very rare exceptions, the consumer pull was strong enough, the trademarks good enough, and the front panel decent enough that they didn't really need to explore why. The velocities

---

58. AC Nielsen Scantrack, Total U.S., xAOC, 2016 calendar year, quad week ending 12/31/2016; n=16,000 premium brands. Analysis courtesy of The Hartman Group, Inc. The cut-offs in this diagram are measured in POS annualized sales totals, not company-level sales. The typical brick-and-mortar markup is about 90–100% of your per-unit list price; exceptions include businesses selling mostly to Costco and/or other retailers who do not use distributors.

themselves won over additional accounts. But . . . you are much more likely to go through a learning curve like Halo Top's. Cute halo lids by themselves do not create unicorns in CPG.

Founders who have scaled exponentially treated the market as a rolling, semi-controlled experiment. Sometimes, it was a very fast-moving experiment (SkinnyPop). Other times, it was much slower (siggi's). Almost every time, though, consumers grabbed the brand off the shelf at ever-growing rates per store. For some premium CPG brands offering weightier innovation, it simply takes a longer approach before you can feasibly get up the quarter-pipe Ramp.

I meet an inordinate number of CPG founders who are simply selling, selling, selling into retail accounts. They are caught up in a distributor's view of the universe: move volume . . . somewhere, anywhere. They act like suppliers, and end up working for brokers and distributors and retailers. Ugh.

I also meet founders trying desperately to avoid the financial headache of distributor-based, go-to-market paths. These folks end up picking e-commerce or direct-ship retailers, so they, too, can stay happily ensconced in a B2B operation, where *their* view of their brand is the only one that they see every day. It's more comfortable not to listen to your consumers or to even ask for their feedback. Very comfortable. When these alternative-channel founders begin to look at brick-and-mortar—because they realize scale is maxing out online— they get pale-faced, very quickly. Double ugh.

Without a self-critical, experimental mindset, you will scale your "growing" B2B business into retail blindly. This has led to many a stalled brand at the level where, ironically, companies begin to qualify for institutional capital.[59] They either don't get funded, or if they do obtain a Series A round, they squander much of it because the business was not actually set up for acceleration. Triple ugh.

By running your CPG startup like an aggressive, rolling experiment in the early years, you can also properly frame distributors, brokers,

---

59. I define *stalled* as growing between the rate of inflation and the rate of the natural/organic sector in general.

retailers, and everyone else as support staff. This puts you cognitively and emotionally "in charge" and, if you can sustain this perspective, allows you to make cool, calm, and collected strategic decisions as the experiment unfolds. Conversely, if you're acting desperate for scale, industry stakeholders will sense this and take advantage of it.

The real value of launching your startup in this way is that you're admitting upfront that your initial UPC mix is simply a rough draft and using consumer feedback to tweak the mix. Not everything about it may be off; it may be the pricing, or hero ingredient, or assumed consumer audience, or flavor profiles, or package design, or pack sizes, or channels, etc.

The problem with looking at a CPG business as an experiment, though, is that it's not actually possible to run a CPG business like a strict laboratory experiment, where you painstakingly isolate variables across the 4Ps. That would be nice. It is certainly the fantasy encouraged by marketing science. Instead, you must learn to diagnose problems with direct measurements and with a large dose of inference in order to form an updatable, real-time symptom map of the business. You also cannot pause the business as you evaluate it, as one could in a laboratory study.

I advocate using three basic principles to guide an experiment aimed at riding all the way up the Skate Ramp growth curve:

1. Set an aggressive but realistic pace to $1 million in gross sales.
2. Pay attention to all your key performance indicators.
3. Throttle carefully early on.

Pace Aggressively, but Realistically, to $1 Million

One million in gross sales sounds like a lot when you've just started and are selling at a $2,000 per month run-rate. I get it. And it won't happen in a year for most founders. In my experience, a founder new to the industry and executing a well-run launch can pull this off in two to four years, on average.[60] This number puts you comfortably over the line into Phase 2 of the Ramp, so you have enough trailing sales to analyze the health of the business.

As you run your initial market experiment, you can't focus only on sales and gross income. You must also focus on consumer acquisition (like any good tech firm would). Your primary customer may be a retailer, but they are not driving the experiment. They are simply a gatekeeper. As a CPG startup, your experiment is happening on kitchen counters, on sofas, in car cupholders, and on office desks. Never forget this. Consumers are the oxygen that create and sustain your cash flow.

So, how many consumers does it really take to generate $1 million in trailing, annual sales?

If we assume a mock list price of $2 per unit, we're talking about 500,000 units annually. Again, this total sounds unattainable at the start, when you are hand-packing stuff. But trust me, it's very possible. Hundreds and hundreds of CPG start-ups have gotten there.

But if you need to sell to 500,000 consumers each year to sell your 500,000 units, your business is an abject failure. That would be a 100 percent trial business. With 100 percent rejection. Ouch. Believe me, 95–100 percent rejection has happened many times before in the CPG industry. Many times. And it may take you more than a year to figure this out if you don't pace your growth in retail accounts. Glad-handing, over-eager brokers can get you sucked into an amazing topline growth illusion that collapses fast on the back end, like a bad prom date with two left feet. You can't dance? Next! Meanwhile, you will be so distracted with production in order to service your illusory growth that you may not even notice the dwindling reorders.

---

60. AC Nielsen Scantrack, Total U.S., xAOC+C channels, past five years, quad week ending 11/21/2015. Analysis courtesy of The Hartman Group, Inc. In a random sample of launches referred to earlier, only 3–5% of premium food/beverage brands attained $1 million of cash register sales in their first 12 months.

If you don't have repeat purchase, you are dead in the water in most CPG categories—those that are also known as *fast-moving consumer goods* (FMCG). Lack of repeat purchase means your line failed the primary memorability test. Congratulations! You are officially an interchangeable commodity, like those crappy, nearly unbranded, clear bags of mixed nuts and candy at the convenience store. Branding agencies will prey on you like vultures. "You need a killer story, and I got an A in English literature." The good agencies, though, will actually avoid a hopeless case with too many fundamental problems. (More on this in Chapter 7.)

Most CPG brands generate 70–80 percent of their sales from 20–30 percent of their consumers due to the phenomenon of repeat purchase.[61] Following this highly generalized average, we can see that a healthy CPG brand selling-in once a week to heavy repeat users and maybe three times a year to everyone else (as many successful premium, RTD beverages do), you need only 50,000 consumers annually to create a $1 million business. (Figure 11) This is a tiny little "tribe" inside a country of 329,000,000 people.[62]

Repeat-purchase variation for any product line is a much more drawn-out continuum than this, but bear with me here. I'm oversimplifying to drive home a larger point. If you take the number 50,000 and imagine spreading it evenly around the country, parallel to a large national chain retail launch (e.g., Target or Kroger), you can see how incredibly thin your $1 million in sales could easily be spread in terms of consumers per square mile or consumers per store.

The top metropolitan areas in the United States each have a median population of one-million people.[63] That means our mock CPG brand has to reach only 5 percent of the local population in one me-

---

61. This truism has been debated by marketing scientists, since the ratios depend on the time period in which repeat purchase is measured. But you may want to read *Superconsumers: A Simple, Speedy, and Sustainable Path to Superior Growth*, by Eddie Yoon (Harvard Business Review Press, 2016), for more on why CPG brands tend to display this pattern again and again.

62. https://www.worldometers.info/world-population/us-population/. Based on United Nations estimates as of August 31, 2019.

63. U.S. Census. Premium Growth Solutions analysis.

Figure 11: The Cash-Flow Value of Heavy Buyers

# Consumers	Annual Buy Rate	Unit Price	Revenue
10,000	40	2	$800,000
40,000	3	2	$240,000
			$1,040,000

dian population city to earn $1 million. If the $1 million comes from combined sales in a few regional metros, the local population-share burden only declines.

Wow! Five percent. And only 1 percent need to become heavy users, at one per week—not even daily users.

Which scenario sounds easier for your marketing director?

Scenario A: Generate 10,000 heavy users in one city—many of whom might work, party, and/or live together or otherwise have overlapping social networks.

Scenario B: Generate 10,000 heavy users sprinkled all over the top 20 cities and, more importantly, spread very thinly in any given social network within those cities.

You may have an instinctual answer, but pause and think about it some more. I'll circle back to this topic in Part Three.

Track Your Growth-Driving KPIs

Although CPG founders get schooled awfully quickly these days about maintaining strong velocities, that is not the only KPI you should be tracking as you ramp toward $1 million.

Velocity growth can occur for years in the exact same stores—*if* you have a scalable proposition not tied to a narrow cult (e.g., kale chips). (Figure 12) In the vast majority of Skate Ramp case studies I've reviewed, velocities grew all the way up to $100 million in sales

Figure 12: Steady Velocity Growth Is Possible for Years

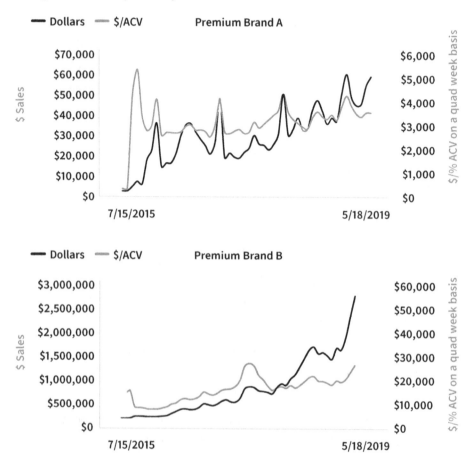

and well beyond that point in many cases, though certainly not always.[64] (Figure 13)

Many folks new to the industry do not understand that the exponential growth typical of Skate Ramp brands can theoretically be created simply by doubling average velocities over time (i.e., from 5 units U/S/W to 10 U/S/W sold per store, per week). This velocity increase may be driven by only 15 percent of selling stores, leaping to

---

64. AC Nielsen Scantrack, Total U.S., xAOC channels, past four years, quad week ending 5/18/2019.

Figure 13: Velocity Growth Puts a Brand on the Skate Ramp

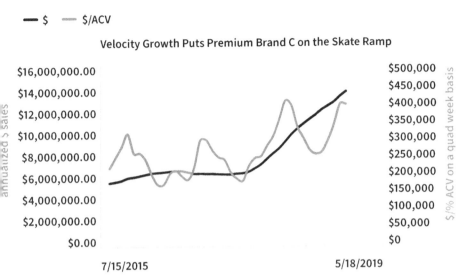

— $ — $/ACV

Velocity Growth Puts Premium Brand C on the Skate Ramp

20+ U/S/W at top-performing stores, while others do not even accelerate to 10 U/S/W.

Would your field salespeople notice the change? They should, but they might not if it is a slow creep, which it often feels like at the store level. They should eventually notice going from half a case to one or two cases a week at high-traffic stores. If it takes more than a year for this growth to happen (which is common), though, it may sneak up on them. You are not going to see average velocities go from 5 to 30 or 40 U/S/W within a couple of years in anything but a unicorn scenario.

However, even modest changes in the slope angle of velocity (U/S/W or $/%ACV) have a huge effect on the topline curve across thousands of stores. When combined with increased distribution at new stores full of predisposed consumers, things can get exciting. The effect of velocity growth is much like any compound interest calculation. The larger the door-count balance on a premium-priced CPG business, the more small changes in YoY average velocities rapidly accelerate topline sales. Yum!

It is easy to be pessimistic about velocity growth, since it is much rarer than you might think for in-demand, premium CPG goods. What pessimists don't factor in, though, is what Skate Ramp brands tend to exhibit and sustain:

- Healthy, viral repeat-purchase rates
- A reachable, enthusiastic fan base (i.e., e-mail lists, IG/FB followers, etc.)

These are the two under-discussed KPIs that indicate the above-average memorability required to grow exponentially.

Repeat Purchase

Ultimately, an initial year one repeat-purchase rate of 50+ percent on an annual basis is very possible for successful premium CPG brands.[65] (In contrast, the typical BigCo product launch averages 11 percent annual repeat!)[66]

It is challenging to directly measure repeat-purchase rates on small CPG businesses. If you have seven figures of revenue in a large metro, there is an online survey trick that can potentially work.[67] Direct repeat measurement in the early millions is not crucial, though. That's because the primary KPI—velocity—can be used to infer repeat well enough for strategic-planning purposes.

The best inferential metric for establishing the existence of strong repeat purchase is to measure *velocity growth* at the same stores for more than a year. When velocity is growing, it is almost always be-

---

65. Here "repeat" means at least two purchases in 12 months. My sources are confidential and · anecdotal. E-commerce brands tend to perform well on repeat because of their ability to create direct relationships through scientifically testable marketing communications.

66. https://www.catalina.com/news/press-releases/less-than-1-of-shoppers-drives-sales-volume-for-the-typical-new-cpg-product-says-report-from-catalina/

67. This "trick" involves gathering a very large number of local shoppers at retailers where you are selling-in to take an online "river" survey through a platform like Google. If you can get a large-enough base of complete responses, you can actually measure the statistically meaningful variation between small numbers. The rest is my little secret for now.

cause trial is adding sales on top of a stable repeat-buyer base (consuming at varying levels of repeat, of course).

But don't get too excited, because velocity growth for three to six months doesn't mean anything by itself, unless it's crazy fast. (Hang on tight to that unicorn mane!) One of many reasons a few months of velocity growth isn't indicative of true growth is operational. You probably haven't stabilized your shelf presence/out-of-stock percentage during this early window as a small, undercapitalized company. To be sure, you really need 12 to 18 months of data (depending on its granularity). So, don't sloppily enter accounts thinking you can get out of them fast with some magical, fast-twitch velocity test early on. Not wise. It could be a giant waste of inventory and damage relationships with the trade.

Reachable Fan Base

Your most important influencers are your current repeat buyers. Not all of them are the extroverted, brand-ambassador type. Enter social media, where even the introverted fan feels comfortable talking you up.

Using e-mail harvesting, IG/FB, Snapchat, and Twitter to build a digital fan community during the early years is more important than ever. *But wait. I thought only a smidgen of organic posts ever get seen by followers?* True, the organic viewing rate is typically low, if not getting worse all the time. But paid ads to followers work quite well—if your product line has strong consumer engagement. The point of building fan communities is *not* to have some intense, backyard-pool dialogue with your consumers. Sorry to say, but most consumers have no interest in dialoguing with you, per se, unless there's a problem. Not even your fans. Consumers have hundreds of brands they repeatedly purchase. Don't count on being the one they choose to like and to comment on constantly. Might happen. Probably won't.

The power of your digital community early on lies less in brand-building and marketing return-on-investment (ROI) than it does on allowing you to do episodic, scrappy, paid consumer research on your repeat buyers. This admittedly biased sample (of your repeat buyers) allows you to move beyond overly affirming anecdotes that founders subconsciously cling to, per the human Law of Confirmation Bias.[68]

The farther you move along your in-market journey, the harder it will be to accept that fundamental aspects of your business are completely messed up. If you've been selling giddily without measuring in a way that will surface a problem objectively, will you even have time to listen for the signals of a major problem?

In CPG, the largest source of confirmation bias—what I call *founder myopia*—is the product itself. Assuming your first iteration is the one that will scale makes no sense without some good, fresh market evidence to support that assumption. When asked and provided with an easy way to communicate with you, your fans can clue you in on minor or major issues for which they are quietly forgiving you. In fact, when the desired outcome is compelling, early fans may cut you way too much slack, but the next waves of consumers probably won't.

If you can't generate an online gathering-place full of repeat buyers (e.g., Instagram or Facebook) reasonably fast, despite incentivizing them to do so, this is your first warning sign. If you have a reasonably sized community of 2,000+ followers (all platforms), you can execute research to optimize your product line *and* to understand why fans are coming your way.

You will need at least 250–300 repeat buyers (preferably more) who can weigh in on:

- Why do they like your product line. Is the motivating outcome scalable?

- Who are the "wrong" consumers"? (i.e., those motivated by non-scalable outcomes or who make insincere trade-offs on taste)

---

68. I highly recommend *Mistakes Were Made (But Not by Me): Why We Justify Foolish Beliefs, Bad Decisions, and Hurtful Acts*, by Carol Tavris and Elliot Aronson (Mariner Books, 2015).

- How do they use it in everyday life? Does it fold well into their daily routines?

- How often do they use it? (e.g., daily, weekly, special occasions)

- What, if anything, they would change? (e.g., weird after taste, pack size, etc.)

If you field a top-posted survey to your Instagram followers and can't even get 100 completes in a three-day period, despite having thousands of followers, this is your second warning sign. (I recently had a client with this issue.) Paid influencers are very efficient at taking your money and then adding bogus followers who are not consumers to your follower count. I call it *aspirational following*. Twitter is essentially built on the aspirational following of celebrities and brands. But it happens on every social networking platform.

––––––––––

Guess what? You don't need to be an e-commerce or direct-to-consumer (D2C) brand to incorporate these two under-discussed KPIs: repeat purchase and reachable fan base. However, the most reliable way to examine them is to have an e-commerce business as a portion of your revenue. It serves as an ideal consumer research laboratory that can be used to indirectly assess the why and what behind your early topline performance.

Remember, in the first $1 million, you are not trying to measure either of these sophisticated KPIs with the laser-like precision of a BigCo brand. Nor can you, because no third-party, general-population data source could find enough of your ultra-small brand's consumers.[69]

––––––––––

69. Nielsen, IRI, and SPINs all have consumer panels. Unfortunately, they usually require your business to be larger than $15 million in order to find more than a qualitative sample. Numerator is a consumer data provider that allows repeat purchase measurement for smaller, seven-figure brands. They, too, cannot find you early on, but they can find you earlier than the established panels I just mentioned. https://www.numerator.com/infoscout-omnipanel

Throttle Carefully

The third principle of managing a small, early experiment is to throttle up very carefully. This is primarily to prevent you from growing
distribution at a rate at which too large a proportion of sales are driven
by initial trial at new doors before you've fine-tuned your playbook to
drive repeat purchase.[70] (More on this in Part Three.)

The goal of throttling carefully is not to prevent unicorn growth
from occurring—although, as I've explained previously, that is mostly
a feature of product design. You'll literally know within a few weeks
of having your brand in brick-and-mortar whether (or not) you have
unicorn-level design. SkinnyPop figured it out in 48 hours, apparently.
New CPG brands don't go out of stock in 48 hours!

The goal is to prevent you and your team (brokers included) from
chasing growth through distribution and thereby faking your topline
experiment, which is super easy to do. It's even easier when an investor hands you $1 million too early in your own learning curve. That's
my only watch-out around taking corporate VC money or large angel
rounds in the first couple years. Save those valuable checks for later,
when you're ready.

Founders who scale fast through angel-funded over-distribution
are trying to act like BigCo, without having the substantial marketing
resources and enormous omni-channel skills of a BigCo sales team. I
call it a *half-assed CPG launch.* Ironically, one of the reasons so many
BigCo line extensions fail is a lack of well-rounded resources brought
to bear on a near instantaneous national roll-out.

The guardrails I recommend on initial throttling below $1 million
in trailing revenue are as follows:

- **Concentrate on building local/regional distribution.** Keep
  stores within a confined geography where you can keep
  in-store fundamentals on track (i.e., not undermine your

---

70. Repeat purchase needs to be sustained to indicate a strong offering. Although consumers
cycle in and out of premium brands, they do stick to better ones for years at a time, if my ethnographic research experience is representative.

experiment with issues like out-of-stocks). It also condenses your early consumers into a geography where you can frequently meet them in person and where existing, high-intensity, offline social networks accelerate local formation of your online fanbase.

- **Get to $250,000 as fast as possible**—without entering a strategically foolish channel or banner (i.e., Walmart). At this point, limiting YoY growth doesn't matter, unless it is foolishly executed and bursts your capacity to fulfill. You need to have some kind of local/regional critical mass to get the engine running on operations and to get trial going at a decent clip. This phase involves a ton of work. It's not a hobby. It is especially painful in a business that is brick-and-mortar only.

- **Avoid growing more than 200 percent YoY in the first year or so after you hit $250,000.** This is the throttling part. You're new to the Skate Ramp. And staying on it isn't easy. Again, if velocities are phenomenal, you and everyone else will quickly know it, and you will easily attract the money to ride your cutesy unicorn all the way up the Ramp. Then, you will burn this book and give endless podcast interviews about how no one needs expert advice from punks like me.

Throttling, therefore, consists of an initial operational surge followed by the judicious constraint of new distribution to a level that permits exponential growth but does not lead to over-distribution. If your topline is growing by more than three times annually and your velocity is not growing, you are simply buying growth through distribution. I hope you're rich. This is how folks *try* to ride the Skate Ramp but then usually fall on their skate-rat behinds.

The Chief Benefit of Closely Managing a Small Experiment

There's a much more important reason why you need a small, controlled experiment in the journey to $1 million. You need to discover *why* you're growing or not growing. You need to understand the why behind your growth no matter how awesome you're doing on the ramp to $1 million, not only if you're struggling. Even the unicorns should figure this out as they launch vertically.

Let me share a story.

I once got more or less smartphone-chased (is that a thing?) by a venture capitalist at the summer Fancy Food show in NY. I didn't understand his urgency, but with investors it usually revolves around needing a third-party perspective on a problem child in the portfolio, plus a big dash of banker impatience. After the usual stop and go of trying to find a mutual time and place at a trade show, we hooked up near the end of floor hours, next to the by-then empty registration counters.

The first words out of his mouth were, "Hey, James, great to meet you. Can you come by our booth? I want to show you a brand I'm working with."

I liked his intensity and directness. To match it, I turned on 100 percent pure James and replied, "Great. Let's go."

As we walked toward the booth, he told me the story of the founder's accidental success. I listened quietly and nodded. When we reached the booth, the brand ambassador team was packing up for the day, and my investor friend asked for some samples.

"Where can we sit?" he asked.

I suggested the meeting table in an empty nearby booth.

Before I was even in my seat, investor guy blurted out, "So, we want to make sure we can continue this growth. And I was wondering how you work with brands?"

"Do you know why you're growing?" I tossed off casually.

Silence. . . . "Why we're growing," he slowly repeated as he chewed on what seemed to be a new question.

"Well, who's buying the product?" I asked.

"Everyone. Literally everyone," he stated enthusiastically, as if this was meaningful validation of something.

"I'm sure it feels that way, but that doesn't help us understand why seemingly disparate people are buying the brand. You'll want to dig into the most scalable why you can find among them."

Wheels started to turn inside investor guy's head.

I had to give this newer CPG investor cred for wanting more perspective on why they were growing so well. It showed a healthy skepticism that all founders need to maintain as they succeed. The problem is that too many founders ask why only when the shit is hitting the fan.

If you hit the gas too early and start buying distribution non-strategically (like a big, hasty CPG line extension), you will not have given yourself the time to figure out the why that will fuel your experimental iterations. (See Chapter 7.)

So, how can founders better understand the why behind their business as they run their small experiment?

That will depend in part on the channels in which you are launching (the specific tactics and tools of which are beyond the scope of this book).

The key to understanding why you are, or are not, growing or growing quickly and sufficiently enough is to get at the very symbolic dynamics that I discussed in Part One—namely:

- What attribute-outcome associations are your early consumers holding in their minds?

- Which associations do your heavy buyers hold?

- Which of these attribute-outcome associations is the most scalable?

- If none of them feel scalable, what are your consumers *not* perceiving that could unlock a connection to a scalable dietary outcome?

- Is the result of this research very different from why you started the company and why you get up in the morning to run it?

In premium CPG, there is often a huge sophistication gap between the founder and even early repeat buyers. This could be culinary sophistication in terms of flavor design, or it could be based on an incredibly deep knowledge of specific health issues related to diet and nutrient intake. Orthomolecular nutrition? Seriously, what is it again?

The amount of knowledge the average premium CPG consumer wants to ever acquire about your product is remarkably low. This is as true for Lay's potato chips and SkinnyPop as it is for kale chips and aloe juice.

You will hear lots of folks at Expo West muttering, "If only we had more money to educate our consumers about why this is so important for them, we could nail it!" Hold on. What exactly do you want to educate them about?

Many a premium CPG founder has become so lost in their own "expert" view of their product and its most sophisticated nuances and consumer outcomes that they actually correct their consumer fans at trade show booths and field-marketing events. Corrections? Are you kidding me? Please shut your pie-hole and listen.

If someone is buying your product weekly or twice a week, they don't need to be corrected about anything. Instead, you need to communicate *with* them to figure out why they are buying it repeatedly. Then, you need to accept that it may have little to do with the obscure knowledge set you used to develop the product to begin with. Responding to consumer "ignorance" with founder condescension is an ironically small-stakes version of the kind of arrogance that has led many BigCo brand teams to drive their brands into a ditch.

Repeat consumers don't need to "get it." Founders do. If we return to the case of siggi's, Siggi Hilmarsson was passionate about introducing skyr to the American public. The primary impetus was his personal distaste for processed American yogurt.[71] Yadda, yadda, yadda. Who cares? I can tell you for a fact that he didn't start out trying to preserve the waistlines of well-heeled Manhattan singletons. Not at all. It was his early repeat consumers who clued him in on his product's low-sugar count and the powerful sensory cue of this low sugar count: extreme tartness.

The vast majority of premium CPG consumers don't want to be geeks. They want to consume the products of geeks in a simple and convenient form. Consumer packaged goods are all about easy-to-shop, easy-to-buy, easy-to-use shortcuts to achieve desired outcomes. Find the right way to sell to consumers, not the right way to turn them into you. If Narcissus was around and could ride a Skate Ramp today, he'd fall off right away because he would be taking a damned selfie halfway up. You do not want to be a $10 million company that has spent so little time listening to consumers that you inadvertently spend a lot of money marketing your own personal "why" in order to drive organic growth. Oops.

---

71. https://www.inc.com/articles/201102/siggi-hilmarsson-founder-of-icelandic-milk-and-skyr.html

CHAPTER 7

DISCIPLINED 4P ITERATION

O K. You are armed with your three key KPIs: generating growing same-store velocities, a dense core of heavy repeat buyers, and throttled growth between $250,000 and $1 million. You are a learner. An experimenter. Humble. Hungry. Pumped. You are no longer a hobbyist. In fact, if you're selling more than $500,000 annually, you've already beaten 80+ percent of your peers. You rock.

Now, it is time to plan your 4Ps like a CPG pro. It's also time to do annual or semi-annual diagnoses of the business's progress along the Ramp.

I know it's trendy for the ambitious founder to study hip strategy books (e.g., *The Innovator's Dilemma, Purple Cow, Blue Ocean Strategy, Your Strategy Needs a Strategy*, etc.). But guess what? In consumer packaged goods, nothing has ever been proven wrong with the 4Ps of strategic planning: product, place, price, promotion. (Figure 14) It's just that the process of 4P planning can tempt operators to (a) avoid establishing a clear competitive strategy and (b) drown your team in tactical minutia. I certainly see many founders diagnosing their business amidst the tactical weeds. *It's the front panel! It's the Facebook campaign! It's the flavors!* Whoa. Not so fast.

In my work with clients, I encourage them to craft a strategy executed with a competitively different mix of 4P moves that their com-

Figure 14: The 4Ps of Strategic Planning

Product	Placement
<ul><li>Product design</li><li>UPC portfolio design</li><li>Package design</li><li>NFP/label information</li><li>Supply chain</li><li>Manufacturing</li></ul>	<ul><li>Channels and specific accounts</li><li>Merchandise department(s)/ key buyer</li><li>Shelf placement (where in planogram)</li><li>Ancillary placement(s) (i.e. end caps shippers)</li><li>Account specific UPC portfolios</li></ul>
Promotions	**Price**
<ul><li>Social media</li><li>Field marketing</li><li>Paid online ads</li><li>Paid physical advertising</li><li>PR</li><li>Trade displays</li><li>Trade advertising</li><li>Price discounts</li></ul>	<ul><li>Price per unit (to manage price perception w/ consumer and lift net profits)</li><li>Price/pack architecture by channel/account</li><li>Baseline vs. promoted unit pricing</li></ul>

petitors aren't using and probably *won't* use (think Sun Tzu). This approach to strategy is based on studying what existing national and rising star players are currently doing to grow. Sometimes it might mean scaling to seven figures regionally on the basis of being a local brand before spreading one's national wings with a suddenly very different killer positioning.

Whatever strategy you develop to compete in the marketplace, successful brands always iterate their strategy when the KPIs go south. They do this by studying their core operating category across key channels and then dispassionately diagnosing the most likely largest source of underperformance and its relationship to key decisions.

I see so many new founders do the opposite. They get caught up in reactive, anxiety-fueled tweaking. They tweak so many things in a nervous string of small moves that it causes too much signal noise underneath the KPIs, preventing founders from seeing what worked or what didn't work six to twelve months later. The experiment has become completely uncontrolled.

Yes, a CPG brand experiment is not a true laboratory experiment, but it can be a controlled one. Non-systematic diagnosis is the leading source of poor strategic planning in early-stage brands. You need to be as careful *not* to change tactical moves that are working as you are to change tactics that aren't working—especially if you want to ride the Skate Ramp.

Despite the need for care, big tactical changes work best with consumers, especially when the change is strategically concentrated on just one of the 4Ps. Think of the dramatic pack redesigns of Halo Top and RXBAR. Minor tweaking across the 4Ps is a classic sign of strategic hesitancy and risk aversion. Consumers just don't notice small tweaks in anything other than unit pricing, and the ideal premium CPG consumer early on is not one who cares much about saving 20 percent in your category (although they'll certainly take a discount if you hand it to them).

If your revenue growth is not 75+ percent YoY, you're not on the Skate Ramp. If your growth is even more shallow, it might as well be linear. Although a growth rate of 15 percent YoY is much faster than the total CPG market overall, it is a slow crawl to scale. Investors may very well give up on you if it continues too long.

Even if you are growing exponentially it may not be sustainable. If same-store velocities stagnate quickly or start declining, you have a real issue. These are signs that you are faking it with distribution growth and are not going to make it up the Ramp. In skate rat terms, this is like the punk-ass who kicks really hard just before she hits the ramp and then lands on her ass anyway.

In my experience, there is a master prioritization critical to diagnosing why you are not riding the Skate Ramp or not riding it properly (i.e., bad technique). This prioritization is based on what most drives intense repeat purchase and high conversion from non-buyer to moderate/heavy buyer among a properly predisposed consumer audience in CPG.

Here's how I diagnose brands in these situations. (Please give it a try yourself and see if it helps your decision-making process.)

1. I always **begin with Product**, analyzing the consumable substance and the package. A poorly designed innovation is not going to gain much from a channel-optimization effort or from advanced pricing analytics.

2. Next, I **assess Placement**, including channel mix, banner mix, and in-store positioning. Raw kale juice and Walmart Supercenters are not a capitalist marriage made in heaven.

3. Then, I **examine Pricing** in top-volume channels, including the design and performance of temporary price reductions (TPRs).

4. Finally, I **look at consumer Promotion**, including promotional programs in high-volume channels and promotional activities in key strategic markets. It's not that promotion is the last thing to turn on. It's that it's the last place to look for a problem or a source of hidden growth.

In my experience, this is the relevant pyramid of causality affecting CPG velocities (Figure 15), because it prioritizes for founders what most influences the consumer and their likelihood of converting into a repeat buyer. And, if it hasn't been obvious so far, it is the *consumer* who ultimately determines who rides the Skate Ramp and stays on it.

Now, let's look at each of these four components of iteration, drawing on what we learned in Part One but now thinking of founders running their initial market experiment.

Figure 15: Causality Pyramid in CPG Iteration

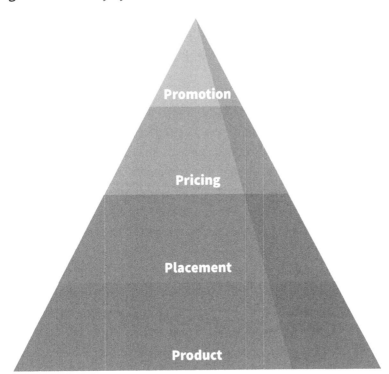

Product Iteration

Unfortunately, product is the most commonly overlooked source of underperformance in new CPG brands—especially the consumable good in the package. Package symbolism is a close second. Both are something you want to get right before you have unwittingly spread half-assed, *meh*-tasting, confusingly labeled UPCs from Seattle to Miami in four different channels.

Yes, it is possible to pivot on product after a national roll-out. But it could take many months for the new product to replace the old, depending on how slowly it is moving in some of your channels and accounts. If it's a major reformulation, it could necessitate switching co-manufacturers. Gulp.

The odds are slim to none that the UPCs you first sell are, across all consumer touchpoints, precisely what will ramp well over the long term. Trust me. SkinnyPop, Caulipower, Chobani, and other similar brands that scale immediately out of the gate strike me as pure anomalies.

Why do I make a big deal about this?

Most founders do not have experience in industrial-scale food and drink formulations. A commercial kitchen formula is *not* proof of concept that your product is industrially scalable. I wish it were so.

Most founders also do not hire top-shelf CPG branding agencies to design their initial packages and brand identity. Today's market is simply too competitive to tolerate the kind of amateurish designs that send no clear signals past the thalamus and into the consumer mind at the shelf, even after they peruse the package.

The kind of scratch-your-head "natural" product that frequently went to market in the 1980s and 1990s survived primarily because the early consumers were ideologues and not representative of any scalable, addressable market. The consumers of those products were, to put it simply, weird folks. They were happy to put in the extra work of figuring out what "it" was. They hated marketing and branding that looked too slick. After all, these are the people who drove miles and miles just to get to that health food store to shop for basic food items. That extra effort was part of their righteous rebellion against the mainstream food system, the Capitalist Machine, even the Man. Remember, at the time the revolution still was not televised.[72] Peace out.

Founders today have to accept that their initial UPC mix is essentially a beta software test. You won't know precisely what is wrong across all touchpoints until you get it out there, build a community of repeat purchasing fans, and learn the attribute-outcome associations driving scalable repeat purchase.

Let your early fans help you fix the line.

---

72. "The Revolution Will Not Be Televised" is the title of a famous poem and song penned by Gil Scott Heron in 1970. If you're under the age of 40, you may want to check it out, because you probably have no earthly idea what I'm referring to. https://www.youtube.com/watch?v=qGaoXAwl9kw

There are two primary risks with any product iteration:

1. **Tweaking that Affects Nothing:** Making tweaks the consumer is unlikely ever to notice. "You changed *what* about the font shadowing? You lowered the sugar grams from 22 to 20? . . . Huh?"

2. **Virtual Relaunch:** A radical overhaul that loses many of your initial heavy buyers, who haven't fully memorized your trademark yet and were relying heavily on the package's graphic design to find you on each trip to the store.

Let's look at each of these risks in a bit more detail.

The Problem with Tweaking

Tweaks are the result of timidity and, frankly, something I normally associate with BigCo. Too many times I've sat in on endless PowerPoint-fueled torture sessions focused on whether the parent brand should be moved up or down, left or right, or whether the trademark color could switch a few pantones here or there. Increasingly, though, I'm seeing this apparently highly contagious thought-virus spread among entrepreneurs who are supposed to be risk-takers. Come on, folks!

Common examples of tweaking include:

- **Updating the trademark font or font design.** This primarily gets noticed by existing customers, but honestly, they'll probably miss it if everything else looks the same. Nor is it enough of a design change to alter key velocity variables (i.e., how much they will buy). This is not going to create some huge behavioral reaction at the shelf. The only exception I can think of is if you originally used an unprofessionally small font and—voila!—finally made it visible.

- **Obsessing over front-panel certifications/claims.** Among CPG entrepreneurs, this almost always means adding *more* certs and claims to a panel where there are already too many. I call it *feature-itis*. Clutter is deadly to clean, quick-uptake, attribute-outcome signaling. If you display too many symbols on your front panel, your panel doesn't stand out on the shelf. For those consumers who do approach your product, you are throwing away a key source of communications control and allowing one-time buyers many orthogonal reasons to buy you that won't necessarily lead to deep engagement. You feed low-quality trial, clueless trial, random trial, etc.

- **Fussing with your brand story on the back panel** is a great example of overly idealistic tweaking. It is based on the mistaken notion that your consumer is buying a narrative, when they are really buying food, beverages, shampoo, pet treats, etc. The only time CPG consumers are buying a narrative is when they buy books. I don't know how else to say it. Over time, as repeat buyers, they may come to appreciate the back story; they also may not give a rat's petard about it . . . ever. I have yet to see any scientific evidence that brand backstories cause repeat or help sustain it. They are great attention-getters to initially drive trial. But pumping up trial won't solve long-term velocity problems.

The primary problem with tweaking is less what is tweaked than the spirit behind the behavior: *an unwillingness to make a big, bold strategic pivot based on fresh fan understanding.*

Unlike in a precision-obsessed chemistry or a pharmaceutical lab, in CPG you need to wield a big iteration mallet. Otherwise, the consumer just won't notice or react. The consumer is not a molecule in a test tube. They're distracted, impatient, hasty, and assaulted with lame, irrelevant marketing 24/7. Unlike a molecule, they also possess an arrogant human thalamus that shuts out 90 percent of inbound signals all day long. Remember, too, that BigCo outguns you with more shelf-space and communication resources than you would even know what to do with as a new founder.

That is why, if you're going to iterate product, you absolutely need to do something that is visually or otherwise sensorially huge, mongo, big, thunderous. It should also be a research-based decision, not the artistic guess of an otherwise talented graphic designer, copywriter, or suspiciously well-dressed, Tesla-driving agency head. Multiple touch-points may or may not need to come into play.

Virtual Relaunch

The problem with completely redoing almost everything about your product (but the trademark) is that you may lose consumers and you may lose trust with the trade and investors. Look, if there's a critical flaw and you found out too late, sometimes you have to pull the plug and restart. Don't sweat it. But recognize that you will have a major storytelling challenge on your hands. Know your story about why you're relaunching.

Most relaunches follow a failed launch, and the retail trade is very well aware of this sequence of events. So, if you try to portray yourself as the tiny group making huge product changes strategically, you'll still have to battle the relaunching stigma with all your stake-holders. Are you financially prepared for this scenario? Not to mention the fact that you could lose distribution and accounts, if the relaunch is not carefully managed.

Relaunch is probably not even the right term. It's more like "here's my new brand." LinkedIn profiles are chockfull of these stories, if you scroll down far enough. It can work, but you need to keep it to a pro-fessional minimum in a tightly connected trade.

As I mentioned in Chapter 4, the kind of relaunch you desperately want to avoid is one in which the trademark changes. If the trademark is, indeed, most of the problem, then you may have no choice. But it's important to recognize that this is essentially a wind-down. The new trademark (even in the same category) will be considered by all stakeholders, including the consumer, as a completely new brand and company. The fact that the same LLC launched it is immaterial.

The Middle Ground: Bold 1P Iteration

In general, productive iterations to your initial product line can be found in the middle of the continuum between hesitant tweaking and a virtual relaunch.

This middle ground usually focuses on a Halo Top style overhaul of touchpoints within just one of the four Ps, preferably the front panel design and/or product mix. The specific P is less the issue than that it be done within the framework of a data-fueled, competitive strategy. Focusing on product works when there is good reason to believe the issue is *not* the product formulation itself, including your ability to find any meaningful consumer outcomes you can anchor to it. If the issue *is* product formulation, the principles to use are those discussed in Part One.

While there are many Big Mallet approaches to strategizing your ride along the Ramp, I'm going to discuss a less common, but often successful, form of iterating a CPG business. It almost never gets mentioned at any trade events. It involves incubating a *future* product line and winding down the original one, something that is almost never done in BigCo. It isn't done by most CPG brands, because there is often too much cash flow (LittleCo) or base profit dollars (BigCo) at risk in the line that should otherwise be wound down due to poor demand trends. Yet, it has been done before and done recently.

Healthy Choice is a famous frozen entrée brand conceived and spearheaded by a former CEO of ConAgra Foods, after he suffered a heart attack.[73] Now, there's a personal mission. It was one of the most successful CPG brands launched during the "low fat" movement of the late 1980s and early 1990s. But get this: it was a classic frozen TV dinner—a four-compartment tray meal. A *have your steak and eat low-fat, too* kind of thing. By the 2000s, however, the base product line

73. https://www.healthychoice.com/our-story

was declining . . . badly. So, in 2008, the company launched Steamers, its bowl-based brand extension.[74] The last time I checked, Healthy Choice Steamers, Simply Steamers, and Power Bowls represented the vast majority of UPCs in this brand franchise. The migration was carefully managed but at an aggressive pace, because the base Healthy Choice Dinners line has for years created every brand manager's worst nightmare: a continually leaky bucket.

Incubation is a product-mix strategy for birthing a new brand extension that you intend to become the brand's future core product line. This strategy financially permits the original line to be wound down slowly and then completely, rather than just turning it off like a water spigot. A more recent early-stage CPG brand to successfully accomplish this was none other than Spindrift. (Full disclosure: Although I purchase Spindrift by the case, I do not have equity in the company.) Founded as a premium soda brand in 2010, Spindrift cleverly morphed into a premium sparkling water company using the process of brand-extension incubation.

If you are iterating boldly enough, incubation should terrify the living daylights out of you and your team. It is terrifying for most new CPG founders. What if I picked the wrong UPCs to replace the original business? Argh! To make the terror worthwhile, it needs to be a research-based, calculated risk-taking move. Not one based on pure intuition. And, for god's sake, not a speculative agency exercise.

As I mentioned in the last chapter, the initial market experiment you are running is not a laboratory one. Incubation is simply a specific kind of experimentation.

Incubating your future business may also happen accidentally, because you started platforming too early into multiple categories. Hopefully, if only for the sake of your operations chief and accountant, it's only two or three categories. Yikes! If you did launch in too many categories, it is during the run up to your first $1 million in annual gross sales that you want to figure out which one is the hero category

74. https://www.conagrabrands.com/news-room/news-healthy-choice-cafe-steamers-named-no-1-new-food-product-through-mid-year-by-iri-1200235

that can get and keep you on the Skate Ramp. Then, plan to quietly and boldly wind down the others.[75] Remember the Law of Frito-Lay.

Beyond wielding a Big Mallet, founders need to do something very counterintuitive for action-prone entrepreneurs after a major change to their product mix: wait. Wait for enough time to pass so you can look at key KPIs again. As with any product launch, there is a normal operational ramp-up to the shelf itself. But, even after your revised product mix is on the shelf, you still need to give the new line time to do its thing. I'm not suggesting that you be content with sub-minimal velocities that get you delisted. Just don't expect a unicorn to emerge from your distributor or your SPINS Satori data portals right away.

Remember, exponential growth is fast, but not always explosive out of the gate, and it is not based on wacky velocity growth over a short period of time. The buy rate in your category will also dictate the amount of time it takes for you to notice the effect and the degree of patience you need to have.

Placement Iteration

In reality, regardless of how awesome your product is, you will need to steadily add stores as you track your velocity growth in order to ever grow exponentially. In other words, raising your interest rate in small chunks won't do much if the balance in your account remains pitiful.

The key issues to analyze during placement iteration are:

- The value of the accounts you're selling in
- Your discoverability inside the store environment

Strategic Account Progression

As more and more successful, exponentially growing brands know, the two-fold trick to adding optimal-value stores is to:

---

75. This has been established time and again across the grocery stores of America. Drafting is simply a less creative approach to winning, and timing is everything with this approach to scaling.

1. **Only add accounts/stores once existing stores are demon-strating stable velocities or preferably velocity growth.** This requires that your team become adept at forecasting off of granular scanner data pulls. The more granular, the more that mathematics can allow forecasts with less than 24-months of rolling data. Adding consumer research to top off your forecast with behavior-based understanding will add confidence. I recommend it highly. It's cheaper than ever.

2. **Don't just add stores irrespective of product-channel fit, even if you are able to sell into them.** Today, Walmart and Target continue to chase and recruit tiny startups into their systems for a variety of corporate purposes they will never fully disclose to founders. Their primary strategic rationale is to (a) attract/retain more affluent shoppers and (b) keep their chains fresh and modern. This may or may not be a good thing for your business. But historically, no mass retail chain bends over backward for a supplier who produces negligible penny profit due to its tiny scale.

   Getting visibility in the aisles of these huge stores is an enormous challenge. These mass retail chains don't have an established track record of giving brand new brands valuable endcaps or preferred shelving space. And they won't take slotting money to do so, either. Unless you are the next SkinnyPop, launching in mass chains is unlikely to begin or end well, let alone deliver the self-sustaining growth engine you expected and deserve, even it delivers a surge of initial volume. (Learn more about why in Part Four.)

Before iterating your channel mix to solve a growth problem, you first need to think about a few things that are predictive of the channels in which you should be doing OK (assuming your product offering has been fine-tuned for exponential growth):

- How innovative is my offering in the national category context?

- How many aggressive look-a-likes do I have regionally?

- Is there a sensory trade-off that I'm deliberately asking the consumer to make?

- How much capital can I realistically spend to pay for high visibility placement, wherever I choose to go?

In looking at successful Skate Ramp brands since the 2008 Recession, I've found four major channel progressions that work and have been used. Each path orients to specific macro-classes of innovation and/or capital situations.

1. **The Mass National Path:** Launch nationally via elite supermarkets (e.g., Kroger, HEB) and select Costco divisions. Then, spread both upmarket and down-market from there, based on KPIs and seed capital access.

    Why do it?

    › Ideal for super-simple innovations that ask for no sensory trade-offs and connect to massively popular consumer outcomes (i.e., SkinnyPop)

    › Good option if your offering has a very large addressable market right now

    › This is a well-trodden path for the top serial entrepreneurs who have the capital access, expertise in product design, and the network to pull this off quickly.

    Examples: GoGo squeeZ, SkinnyPop, Bark Thins, Halo Top (2.0)

2. **The Traditional National Path:** Launch in natural/specialty stores (e.g., Whole Foods, Sprouts, health food stores, etc.) before moving to mass-market supermarkets upon

initial proof of concept. Up until 5–7 years ago, this was the dominant route to scale that Skate Ramp brands utilized.

Why do it?

› Optimal for innovations that are ahead of the curve by 10+ years and that may require consumer education and/or demand a sensory trade-off

› The role of natural/specialty stores is to drive key influencer trial and credibility for new attributes or attribute-category combinations, but this is really only powerful in specific "hot" markets/cities.

› Can transition to local supermarket chains as quickly as KPIs indicate to accelerate growth and stay on the Ramp

Examples: Vita Coco, Kerrygold, siggi's, Plum, Fever-Tree

3. **Deep Local Penetration, then Expansion:** Start in one metro/regional market using local upmarket channels (specialty and any elite supermarkets), and incubate in a confined social environment for optimal experimentation and iteration. Test multiple-channel exposure locally. Proceed to adjacent market(s) based on the results. Repeat or go national.

Why do it?

› Optimal for newer CPG entrepreneurs in any way uncertain about the organic pull of their offering

› Ideal for innovations that are perhaps 5–7 years ahead of the market (Kind, in 2004)—but not the next siggi's, with its tough sensory trade-off

› Useful for refrigerated food/beverage innovations in risky temperature states

> › Mandatory for late-to-the-national-party local craft brands

Examples: Argo Tea, Stumptown Coffee, Calavo, Chobani (!)

4. **Deep Penetration of Alternative Channels** (Online, Foodservice, Gyms) **and Local Retail, then Expansion:** This is an increasingly popular option for many categories due to the higher gross margins for the operator and the ability to have a much steadier, easier-to-manage path to $1 million.

Why do it?

> › Optimal for newer CPG entrepreneurs who are in any way uncertain about the organic pull of their offering

> › Ideal for beverage and snack innovations 5+ years ahead of mainstream supermarket category trends

> › Well-suited to CPG offerings in any temperature state

> › Ideal for anyone who wants to enter brick-and-mortar with a solid base business in hand and the leverage that provides

Examples: RXBAR, Soylent, Nutpods

Yes, other paths exist. These are simply the most well-trodden and the ones the retail trade are familiar with. The paths can be combined, as you may notice. Generally speaking, however, the more ahead of urban food trends you are, the more you want to lean on one of the last three until you have learned the attribute-outcome associations that will help you accelerate. The more undercapitalized you are, the more I recommend some variant of the final path in the early years.

I should say one thing: I have not found a single, magical channel progression that generates exponential growth. Skate Ramp brands have used all four of the paths I just described. Whole Foods can now be both a waste of time and a necessary launch channel. It depends on the kind of innovation you're bringing to market. In the last five years, specifically, we have seen multiple brands accelerate exponentially by launching in supermarkets or club chains (Costco, Sam's Club, etc.), and then later back themselves into the natural/specialty channels to round out distribution and household penetration.

The dynamics of getting into brick-and-mortar retail today make incubating first and deeply in one city or region the preferred option for most founders, because you are undercapitalized. Today, you can put out national feelers more profitably through Amazon, direct-to-consumer (D2C), and select foodservice channels.

The reason channel progression can and should vary based on the offering is that consumers do not behave the same way in all stores or, more importantly, in all channels. So, while Annie's may be for sale in all channels, how folks shop for boxed macaroni and cheese is not necessarily the same in all channels. Some channels shut down specific shoppers' cognitive tracking of specific categories or classes of category. For example, Walmart doesn't yet trigger a hunt for quality fresh produce or meat in the minds of millions of Walmart shoppers. (More on why this is the case in Part Four.)

Strategic In-Store Placement

Distribution power is not just about geographic availability or proximity to your consumers. It is also about your product's visibility to consumers in stores during their shopping trips.

One of the mistakes often made by premium CPG entrepreneurs is to start lowering their average retail price (ARP) through heavy discounting before they've invested money in enhancing their in-store discoverability at high-traffic locations. This is especially common with founders who are new to the industry and do not visit stores enough before they launch.

Yes, a single-period, end-cap display in Whole Foods nationwide will set you back about 30,000–40,000. Ouch. For the right offering, however, enhanced placement combined with a strategically high-value promotion (see below) will generally pay better dividends than just slashing pricing in the Whole Foods interior aisles (where most of the chain's monthly shoppers never venture).

Even better are shipper displays that drop right onto the perimeter, as long as you have the staff to monitor and replenish stocks and to prevent your displays from becoming free shelving for the retailer's private-label products. (Yes, this nonsense happens.) Shipper displays not only allow you to pre-sell more product in, they also give you an in-store billboard and are proven velocity-growth engines when strategically placed around the store perimeter.

The primary visibility iteration is to get your product into high-traffic regions in-store, so you can see the effect on your store velocities. Remember, once such a program is in place, velocities should continue to grow, based on the phenomenon of word-of-mouth and viral spread of the innovation's appeal in the local shopper base over time. When this doesn't happen, it is a warning sign related to either your channel/account/store locations or your product itself (i.e., the kale chips conundrum). Running out of predisposed consumers at your current premium price points is a common problem when founders enter mass channels or EDLP retailers way too early.

Pricing Iteration

Premium unit pricing at the retail shelf (or online) generally allows CPG entrepreneurs to sell off their books at a premium case-price, relative to their mainstream counterparts in the market. A premium case-price provides critical oxygen for growth in a new premium CPG brand, because it allows for healthy gross margins (40–60 percent), despite having a high cost of goods. Offering high-quality goods for a bargain price is financially nonviable for an undercapitalized entrepreneur.

That's why I cringe whenever I meet founders at Expo West who are intent on selling, right now, to mainstream category consumers (i.e., Walmart shoppers). They usually have no idea how bloody cheap consumers are when they're shopping at Walmart. I call them the *Wrong Consumer.* Wrong for the early years. There is a time to take their money . . . much later on up the Skate Ramp. (See Part Four for more on this topic.)

The primary lesson I've learned from Skate Ramp brands is that you must *sustain exponential growth with a premium average-unit price* (i.e., post-promo), so that you can slowly lower per-package ARP as you scale. (Figure 16) Some call it *relaxing your pricing.* This is critical to maintaining the high pocket price (or gross profit) to fuel your investments across the other Ps.

However, and this is important, price relaxation is a massively powerful growth tool that you, as an undercapitalized entrepreneur, absolutely do not want to use right away.[76] Not at all. If you try to chase near-term volumes by slashing pricing, you will need to raise tons of money to drive growth investments. Even venture capitalists who practice this approach with $10+ million brands would never recommend it to someone starting out. I hope.

The goal of premium CPG pricing iteration is to make sure your velocities are growing at the highest possible ARP. This not only maintains pricing power for the brand as you scale to $100 million; it also frightens off the cheapskates who will happily destroy your pricing power if you try to BOGO yourself to glory (i.e., faking it up the Ramp). This is very different from just setting a super-high unit price or refusing to discount your product ever, like an artisan prima donna. The case studies I've reviewed don't support either kind of naiveté.

If you've arrived at pricing as a potential source of underperformance, you want to look for two primary strategic pricing problems early on in your iteration process:

1. Suggested retail pricing (SRP) is too low (i.e., too close to the category average in key channels).

---

76. Relaxing pricing is a strategy that BigCo will never use, either, because they start at middling or low pricing and then discount from there. In fact, as inflation hits their bottom-line, they negotiate with retailers to "take pricing up" on their SRPs. That's why their average ARPs track inflation, for the most part.

Figure 16: Example of Relaxing Single-Unit Pricing

This graph shows relaxing of single-unit pricing for three Skate Ramp premium CPG brands over a four-year timeframe[77]

2. Average retail pricing (ARP) is too low (i.e., too close to the promoted pricing of category share leaders).

The CPG entrepreneur's most unique growth problem is that they *need* premium SRP unit pricing, so that the pricing ladder from the shelf (SRP) through their list price onto their pocket price allows them to finance operations and growth-related activities. Yet, by occupying a premium-price position, they have alienated the vast majority of category consumers (before these consumers have even reviewed the package symbolism). This is the existential trade-off that every premium CPG founder makes when they commit to higher quality goods.

A premium SRP is critical to something called *price anchoring*. In premium CPG, if you do not anchor your SRP price high enough, you will not be able to fund promotions that move strategic volume into the baskets of high purchase-intent, repeat consumers. Instead, you will lose too much critical oxygen (gross profits) through onboarding fees and manufacturer chargebacks (MCBs), such as promo-related deductions, free-fills, trade marketing fees, on-invoice discounts, etc.

---

77. AC Nielsen Scantrack, Total U.S., xAOC channels, past four years, quad week ending 5/18/2019.

You will also commoditize your premium brand *before* it has even achieved scale.

Have you ever seen those transparent bags of candy (and whatever) with crappy, unreadable stickers on them at the dollar store? Cheap stuff in a bag with an unknown trademark at an average price. Forgettable, even if you do grab a bag. The risk of having a category *average* unit price with an unknown trademark in ordinary supermarkets is that you, too, might be seen as "random stuff in a bag." *Meh*. That may be a CPG business, but it will never grow exponentially.

Increasingly, research is accumulating to support what many of us studying the premium CPG market have long assumed. Within categories, relative price premiums confer a belief that the higher-priced good is, indeed, of higher quality. Researchers have recently discovered that this price perception may even alter taste perceptions in the human brain.[78] It costs the consumer too much for it *not* to taste better. And so, it does. Funniest thing. I've always suspected this personally about the $25+ wine bottles at Costco I keep buying.

It is critical that consumers *consciously* acknowledge a price premium upon first trying your product, because it filters out consumers just looking for "stuff in a bag," whatever the brand. This leaves consumers with more sophisticated purchase intent. These are the folks you want to build your brand around, because it's simply more efficient to build a fast-growing business around relatively price-insensitive consumers in a category. They will buy you on promo *and* off promo. You're part of their regular set of brands. Perhaps you work really well on a specific kind of occasion where stakes are higher in their mind.

This is the rub: we've all been the consumer shopping with sophisticated purchase intent as well as the one who is content with anything we can find. It's about an attitude more than a consumer type.

If you anchor your SRP too high, though, you will find yourself having to constantly promote in order to move product. This may not be financially viable at all, as you will pay for those promoted prices in almost all instances. It definitely won't work if you anchored your

---

78. https://www.pnas.org/content/105/3/1050

Here's a Shocker!

Premium pricing is a *huge* barrier to acceleration because it is a huge barrier to trial in most channels. That's why marketing scientists and experts rarely study premium goods, which many regard as a market aberration. Since most premium-priced CPG brands never scale, this dismissiveness seemed sensible enough—until the number of premium CPG brands crossing the nine-figure threshold began to substantially grow after the Great Recession.

price too high because of extremely high cost of goods, which you are reluctant to reduce for the wrong reasons. (FYI, elitist notions of artisan quality tend to work against all attempts at scale in CPG.)

Threading the needle on optimal pricing is difficult in premium CPG because many key gatekeepers to the shelf constantly push for relentless trade discounts to create volume surges. These predictable surges fatten the wallets of distributors and brokers, but they almost never create long-term growth, let alone Skate Ramp growth, for CPG brands.[79] They do, however, create initial permanent lifts in your baseline when you enter new accounts. It's part of turning on the account, so to speak. After that, proceed with extreme caution.

Aside from monitoring your ARP such that it is not falling too low and killing your premium halo (and your gross profits), pricing iteration should focus primarily on strategies to relax your ARP slowly over time. Pricing should be relaxed very carefully as you monitor KPIs. If consumer feedback from your ideal audience is positive and store visibility is good in high-traffic stores but velocities aren't growing, it may be time to relax pricing a bit. Generally speaking, you want to do this first in channels with broader shopper populations than those found in natural/specialty stores. This is because channels with broad

---

79. Michael V. Marn, Eric V. Roegner, and Craig C. Zawada, "The Power of Pricing," *McKinsey Quarterly*, Issue 1 (2003).

shopper bases have a high proportion of price-sensitive consumers in any given category.

Promotional Iteration

This final section focuses primarily on how to think strategically about interacting directly with consumers to build awareness and trial. This includes a host of consumer outreach and interaction techniques (e.g., earned media, paid ads, field marketing, email marketing, etc.) that Skate Ramp brands have pioneered in the United States CPG market over the past 20 years.

Why am I talking about this cool stuff last? Well, because my consumer research and case study work strongly suggest that a poorly conceived product offering that launches in the wrong channels at a crazy price premium is unlikely to benefit much from consumer promotional expenses. You're not going to get fans to ride elaborate, custom bike floats off riverside platforms to celebrate over-priced kale chips sold in independent health food stores. Sorry.

If you have ongoing consumer marketing activities, you need to deploy the following principles of iteration to support riding the Skate Ramp.

Always Act Locally

For medium- to high-velocity categories or impulse categories, out-of-store field marketing is primarily the best practice. Vitaminwater, Red Bull, Clif, and Kind pioneered most of the tactics currently in use today. And they still work.

The power of acting locally is primarily about face-to-face interactions with consumers. Field marketing is the industry term for this, covering everything from store demos to out-of-store events. It's tactically about driving sampling in highly predisposed social networks of consumers. Strategically, though, it's about your brand being seen as a grassroots part of local life, even if it's sold in multiple cities or nationwide. Consumers want to interact with grassroots brands of premium quality because they confer symbolic power to the user . . . simply in return for possessing them and consuming them. You have to emerge within their social lives to generate this power. You cannot approach them top down like BigCo brands. For them, field marketing that I'm alluding is simply an elaborate form of paid advertising.

Geo-targeted and geo-fenced social media campaigns are an increasingly common way to act locally in the primary art of marketing: awareness building. One behavioral reason for this is that if you can bombard local social networks with multiple impressions, you are more likely to trigger simultaneous awareness among members of real-life social networks. The geographic density of the advertising impressions matters when it comes to stimulating strategic velocity growth.

Iterate Stories about Your Product Experience

Much of your initial consumer-promotion iteration should focus on attribute-outcome symbolic communication that conveys your most scalable "why" as suggested by early consumer research/interactions. That why story can form the kernel of stories about your brand's impact on consumer lives. These are the stories that consumers tell each other. These are the stories that create strong memorability in CPG. They aren't always necessary, though, if the attribute is well understood but unusual in your category. In other cases, storytelling videos and ads can drive home the consumer outcome, without sounding like an ad.

You may wish to spend time spreading these why stories if other 4P levers appear not to be responsible for underperformance or if you simply want to see how much added acceleration the stories can generate—provided you're spending significant sums on marketing. Human brains are built to receive stories (protagonist + plot + outcome) in many different forms, and stories generally create far deeper memorability than the kind of marketing stunts we see at the Superbowl or in Geico commercials.

Although shocking ads are memorable, they utilize extreme behaviors, not stories, to achieve this. If you're selling a low-end service or commodity, shock ads that simply remind a certain percentage of your base to buy your product on the next trip will usually work just fine. Choice Hotels' recent campaign ("Bada Book! Bada Boom!") even mocks advertising focused on outcomes. "Who glows?" You are *not* Choice Hotels. As an entrepreneurial CPG brand, you need memorability with built-in persuasive rhetoric. And persuasion is best achieved via stories about positive consumer outcomes, in vernacular English.

Be Patient

I can't tell you how many founders I meet who make the same mistake non-marketing executives make at BigCo: they expect some kind of near-term sales return on every marketing investment. Marketing activities should focus on building awareness and on motivating trial for early-stage brands. In many but not all cases, the successful marketing campaigns I've studied, big and small, take six months or longer to reap top-line rewards. You have to be patient before killing the experiment. Hell, it took me nine months of daily posting to see any kind of response on LinkedIn.

Marketing is highly effective for smaller brands, because awareness and trial are the tinder of growth. If you are a CPG brand like Oreo, with near 100 percent awareness, you don't have such easy upside. As CPG brands scale in existing stores, it becomes harder to reach deeper into local shopper networks. This is where geo-targeted ads at the next wave of consumers in local areas can really hasten growth that might otherwise come much slower.

———————

Too often, founders who want to iterate simply start looking at the last major tactical decisions they made for the source of underperformance. This is the "recency" bias of the human mind. If you're upset with a friend, it's usually because of something they recently said or did, even if it's part of a longer-term behavior pattern. We tend to project the dynamics of one-on-one human relations onto a phenomenon that is much more complex and multi-causal. Do a disciplined, systematic review of the business each year to force yourself out of recency bias and confirmation bias, both of which plague CPG entrepreneurs. Or, *gasp*, hire an expert to help you do it.

Remember that all iterations of your 4P mix have to be grounded in a clear competitive strategy, and that the strategy itself may need to change as the competitive reality you're selling in changes. The reality of scaling CPG brands is that your strategy for years one through three may be very different from what it will take in years four through six. Competitive reality changes that fast. I use time here instead of revenue phases, because time is what introduces the most critical disruptions you cannot control (i.e., new entrants, category fatigue, existing entrants obtaining large capital infusions, etc.).

As important as it is to iterate across the 4Ps (if necessary) to stimulate and sustain exponential growth, it is critical not to change too many go-to-market variables at once or, even worse, to change your pricing strategy, channel mix, or in-store positioning in a chaotic string of poorly timed plays, without leaving time to understand the effect of each major move. This kind of spastic tweaking will muddle your experiment and teach you very little.

Be strategic. Be disciplined. But iterate with a Big Mallet.

PART THREE

FINE-TUNING THE
CONVERSION PLAYBOOK

PHASE 2 $1–$7M

CHAPTER 8

THE HEAVY USER

n Part Three, I want to take founders deeper into a more nuanced behavioral funnel that Skate Ramp brands have used again and again to generate above-average, medium- to long-term velocity growth (at same stores).

As Part One hopefully made clear, Skate Ramp brands (and unicorns) tend to have an unusually strong attraction to a specific initial consumer audience. In the case of premium foods/beverages, this allure stems from offering an intriguingly modern approach to achieving a high-stakes, but already popular, dietary outcome. Values-driven behavior ties together the audience far more than demographics.

In marketing parlance, these early fans have very strong *purchase intent*. Most entrepreneurial brands need high per-unit SRPs because their cost of goods sold (COGS) and margin requirements necessitate high case-prices to distributors and retailers. For their part, though, consumers see premium pricing *aspirationally*—as a mark of higher quality and as an identity marker within their own social networks.

While there is definitely such a thing as too high pricing, premium pricing is a proven quality-signaling device that drives fast topline growth. You simply need fewer unit sales than Lay's or Oreo to earn the same amount of money. Celebrate that for a second.

OK, enough gloating. We also know that premium pricing turns off most consumers in a category, making it critical that your products reach price-insensitive consumers in the category.

So, how do ambitious CPG founders want to think about their audience?

I will spend this chapter discussing how purchase frequency and the values-led behavioral drivers behind it are the key to effectively recruiting the right kinds of consumer to your premium brand.

A Super Fun Segmentation of Premium Consumers

Four basic kinds of folks don't care much about price in a category: status buyers, hard-core purity buyers, category geeks, and pragmatic adopters.

> **Status buyers:** These folks need their pantry to be culturally elite and want others to know this. This is now common but not universal among post-grad-educated elites and the urban rich in general. Just go to Whole Foods in Santa Monica, River North in Chicago, or downtown Dallas to see for yourself. Lots of fancy beverage buying is driven by this crowd (with or without much knowledge behind their purchases).[80] They aren't especially committed to or knowledgeable of "natural" notions of purity, per se. The only impetus they need to buy is the status-marking triad: premium price, coveted ingredients, and chic design. These folks are less involved in emerging niche outcomes, but they are driven by the top consumer outcomes relevant to each category they buy. If most of their pantry is premium, it's primarily because they can easily afford it, not because they're savvy buyers.

---

80. Status buyers *do* react to deals, which is a problem if you fail to take their money through over-promotion.

Hard-core purity buyers: These folks are a group SPINS calls the *true believers* and claims to be 11 percent of the U.S. population.[81] (My research indicates that purity buyers overlap heavily with status buyers, since purity obsession has been a status marker since agricultural civilization was invented.)[82] The Hartman Group, however, has found that only 8 percent of U.S. adults buy half or more of their groceries in natural/organic form,[83] suggesting that SPINS' true believers segment may be a tad overestimated (or idealistically defined). And only 1.7 percent of U.S. households purchase three-quarters or more of their groceries at Whole Foods, despite Amazon's acquisition and the roll-out of Prime Now home delivery from these stores.[84]

Regardless of the size of this group, they tend to be driven by hard-core ideologies (often social, ethical, and/or environmental). Honestly, I still find the difference between status buyers and purity buyers really hard to discern in real life. Wanting to have the most "pure" or "sustainable" or "healthy" diet possible are all symbolic rationales for obtaining or reinforcing elite social status. It's just that the ideology is the cover story. This is often the case for those who buy all their groceries at Whole Foods, saying "it's for health reasons." The latter is simply a quest for enhanced control over one's individual fate, something that all social elites tend to fixate on much more than others with more pressing problems. Lots of people get cancer and *don't* alter their diet at all as a means to survive. Think about it.

These purity ideologies are also attractive rationales for those *aspiring* to elite social status in the absence of other traditional elite credentials. What I've learned is that the

81. State of the Natural Industry 2019, SPINS
82. https://www.spins.com/whos-really-buying-natural-and-organic-products-unlocking-the-market-with-consumer-segmentation-from-spins-and-iri/
83. Food Shopping in America 2017, The Hartman Group, Inc.; n = 2004.
84. Premium Growth Solutions survey, June 2019; n = 1,500 adults.

humbler the social origin of the consumer, the more likely this kind of pantry-wide conversion is driven by intense
surface ideologies (purity, environmentalism, or health/
longevity) that mask an underlying quest for a back door
to elite social status. For those *without* post-grad degrees or
elite professional identities, food purity ideologies are very
seductive status markers in modern America.

Category geeks: In some categories, there are genuine foodie
and nutrition geeks who buy multiple brands, because category geeks possess a learned, nuanced set of demand drivers.
They fashion themselves as micro-influencers, and some of
them may actually be so. I've interviewed hundreds of these
folks in my career. The majority are actually *not* good at influ-
encing anyone because they tend to come off as a bit cuckoo
to the next rung out. They're often like PhDs who can't translate their academic theory and jargon into ordinary English.
Yeah, I know. I know. Those people are the absolute worst.

Pragmatic adopters: These consumers form the largest addressable market for premium offerings inside any category
or macro-category. They are open to trying new products
that promise high-stakes outcomes of value to them. They
run neutral to positive about trying the modern way of doing
things in CPG categories. They adopt health ideologies pragmatically and less as a quest to obtain or reinforce social status. (This can be determined through rigorous interviews.)
Many of them are relatively normal middle-class folks.

 If your product can make a Halo Top style argument,
they'll happily pay extra and go for it. But they are generally
very selective about the categories in which they buy premium. These folks are driven by cultural trends in healthy
eating, but they are *not* ideologues or status buyers. This
group extends deep into the middle class, where disposable
incomes and cultural habits don't permit upgrading the

entire grocery budget by two to four times or more, like our purity and status buyers.

Ideally, your initial heavy buyers will include a smattering of status buyers and pragmatic adopters. The more obscure the innovation, the more likely you will be selling initially to category geeks and/or purity buyers. If most of your initial consumers sound like my depiction of these two groups, you seriously want to pause and consider how to reposition your offering for broader appeal. It may not always be possible, if the founder simply prefers to sell to consumers like herself.

Although status buyers are not driven by deep knowledge, they generally exhibit far better interpersonal communication patterns than the annoyingly fundamentalist category geeks and the often ideologically shrill purity buyers. I would seriously recruit your brand ambassadors from the status buyers. Look for relatively uncritical support for new modern attributes coupled with a heavy dose of charming insistence. That's how these folks influence their friends. They're very good at it.

Ultimately, pragmatic adopters are more important to planning your long-term growth and conversion funnel than are status buyers. They're always a bigger group. They'll pay more when the outcome is better fulfilled by the new widget you're selling. Make a very pragmatic, outcome-based argument with these folks. Keep the missionary zeal about your purpose and about your "pure" and "righteous" supply chain to your website or back panel. Or just stop talking about it.

The Right (and Wrong) Consumers for New CPG Brands

Premium CPG founders tend to be category geeks, but they must learn how to design products and sell to status buyers and pragmatic adopters if they want to scale fast and scale at all. End of story. In other words, you need to speak not to the geeky hard core who buy premium CPG products exclusively but to a less sophisticated group willing to pay premium pricing.

What I'm describing is not traditional mass-marketing . . . at all. It's somewhere between niche marketing and a Superbowl ad.

It's time to reintroduce everyone to a five-letter word every MBA in America is taught to deploy only as an elitist slur: niche. The word niche is a polite corporate euphemism for a "failed business," with "failed" meaning *failure to scale*. This harsh definition is completely unfair to CPG entrepreneurs, since all large-revenue brands today once operated as tiny market-share players at some point. The fear that the word *niche* spreads is really the lurking fear that your offering has no potential to scale.[85]

This is what everyone wants to avoid. It might even be why you bought this book. "James, please help me avoid becoming the next kale chips, goji berry juice, or spelt grain sandwich bread." I hear you loud and clear.

Marketing science has confirmed that brands grow by growing their household penetration, no matter what time-range you use to calculate that penetration.[86] This is also true for early-stage premium brands. (Figure 17) What this traditional theory overlooks, though, is how few households, in absolute numbers, are required to generate what BigCo views as initial viable scale: $100 million. Turns out, it takes remarkably few in many cases. This is because of the higher repeat-purchase levels within the heavy buyer portion of their businesses, but it's also because premium unit-pricing requires far fewer buyers to generate large revenues.

Again and again, premium CPG brands are scaling to nine figures with less than 10 percent past thirty-day consumption rates in the U.S. adult population.[87]

---

85. Actually, dozens upon dozens of niche food/beverage brands have $10–$25 million in sales but flat toplines. They truly have found a stable revenue niche. Many are built on obscure nutritional propositions that don't appeal to a *growing* number of people, especially when delivered in non-tasty forms. $10–$25 million is pretty damn good if you started out with your personal savings account as capital. I, at least, am impressed.

86. See Byron Sharp's *How Brands Grow: What Marketers Don't Know* (Oxford University Press, 2010) for more on this.

87. These past thirty-day consumers skew toward heavier purchase rates and are not responsible for all of the annual revenue of the brands listed here.

Figure 17: Big Revenues on Low Penetration

	P30 Penetration	2018 $
Lays	26%	$ 10 figures
Diet Coke	17%	$ 10 figures
Oreo's	16%	$ 10 figures
Chobani	11%	$ 10 figures
Simply	6%	$ 10 figures
Clif	5%	$ 9 figures
Kind	4%	$ 9 figures
Spindrift	3%	$ 8 figures
GT's	2%	$ 9 figures
Horizon	2%	$ 9 figures
Hippeas	2%	$ 7 figures
Bobo's	1%	$ 8 figures

As these premium brand examples show, a relatively small monthly penetration of U.S. households can drive serious scale in premium CPG.[88]

What's important to recognize here is that the repeat purchasing core of a premium CPG brand may be very small in the absolute numbers of people early on. Communicating with those early repeat consumers requires careful thought, so you can learn how to create more of them from the constant influx of trial headed your way.

In a world where mass marketing to gain attention didn't cost as much as it does today, you would simply pay the megaphone and build

---

88. Penetration data comes from a June 2019 Premium Growth Solutions survey of these brands; n = 1000. Revenue estimations are based on AC Nielsen Total U.S., xAOC channel sales data for the calendar year 2018 or Euromonitor data for 2018.

awareness, and your penetration would grow through random trial. You wouldn't care that much about your fans.

But you don't have that kind of mega-capital. And you almost certainly don't have the omni-channel, 90 percent ACV distribution levels required to harness mass trial from mass advertising. Moreover, although mass advertising creates awareness fast, it doesn't persuade trial of premium products well, at all. Even if the consumer shows up at the shelf thinking about you, the sticker shock will keep their hands in their pockets. No ad campaign can really change that dynamic in the near-term. Only *cultural* processes of persuasion can make a premium object seem worthy of that premium to consumers who initially rejected it.

Not targeting your entire strategy requires tons of money so you can generate a tsunami that reaches your ideal consumer by chance. Remember, you're not BigCo. You need to spend money not on chasing light buyers at scale but rather in quickly converting light buyers into moderate to heavy buyers. These folks will return many times more cash to your P&L than will light buyers, and they'll form a group from which you can most realistically recruit influencers to continue the conversion process.

In my experience studying premium brands, light/infrequent consumption is often much less related to a poor sensory experience than it is connected to the light buyer's consumption of the brand on infrequent, non-scalable occasions. Either that or light buying is simply induced by excessive use of temporary price reductions (TPRs). The latter are price-sensitive consumers. They are the wrong consumers on which to build a fragile, young, premium brand on a limited budget. You need to actively discourage their contamination of your P&L.

So, how do you aim your strategy at the right consumer audience?

Locate Small Groups with Big Repeat Potential

All complex, modern societies have hundreds of voluntary, organized groups in which common participation is based on shared values and actions. I'm not talking about caste, ethnicity, religion or race. These are pre-modern, largely inherited identities for most of us. In marketing circles, folks like to call these voluntary groups *lifestyles*. It sounds more aspirational and less clinical than *subpopulation* or *consumer niches* to those hopelessly positive American marketing folks. (That line was for my European readers.)

To be useful in strategic planning, though, these lifestyle consumer niches need to be based on highly specific social variables (or combinations of them), not on massive demographic tags. Moms are not a consumer niche. Triathletes are. Men are not a consumer niche. Professional pharmaceutical sales reps are. (Have you met these folks? Whoa.) And don't get me started on the fallacies of generational marketing. The difference between a truly marketable subpopulation and a demographic group is the concept of shared and defended values put into action in small groups. Humans are not hardwired for bureaucracy; we *learn* to function in those systems. We put up with office BS, but we are evolved for small-group bonding. The extended family is the pre-modern historical core of this kind of bonding across all societies. Americans are obsessed with voluntary groups, because, in part, we spend little time with our extended families.

Ramping your brand inside consumer niches (initially) ensures that you can:

- Generate and document the existence of sustained, preferably heavy repeat purchase (and not just endless, frivolous trial or random impulse buying).

- Learn why the product experience is generating repeat, and generate marketing efforts off this core story.

- Have marketing conversations with your consumers that
don't come off as marketing at all. This is because you have
learned how to participate as an ad hoc, authentic mem-
ber of a real, meaningful, interesting human community.
You're not talking with *all* people ages 18 to 30. *Groan.*

- Staff your company with fans! No demo company can
match the authenticity of real fans staffing a sampling
table or field event. Sorry. I've seen hundreds of demos
in stores. Consumers can sniff out way-too-pretty, paid
brand shills right away.

Needless to say, not all consumer niches are as effective in ramping your brand as others. So, don't just pick any trendy tribe and start
handing out samples. Instead, create tons of opportunities to interact
with *any* early consumers (online and offline). Build a digital following that can serve as a consumer research lab—biased intentionally
toward fans. Then, move in to locate the values-driven niches that pop
out as the ones where your offering is super relevant.

The two most reliable classes of social groupings to pick from
are (1) occupational groups and (2) voluntary lifestyle/recreation
groups. These types of social world represent two of the three kinds
of social identity that we proudly perform on a daily or almost daily
basis in the United States today—as follows:

- **Social class:** This is very close to an inherited social identity, but we often believe it is malleable through effort
and some lucky opportunities. Class is experienced subconsciously for most Americans these days, because we
live in highly segregated class bubbles like never before in
U.S. history. We also choose *not* to acknowledge class dynamics, because they are politically incorrect to discuss.
Yet, regardless of how privileged a person might be at
birth, most Americans still aspire to upward mobility.

    Because changing one's social class is a multi-year
project with a low likelihood of success (given the

latest sociological insights), it is *not* a useful voluntary social-identity tag for brand-building. Moreover, it is simply way too vague, despite the very real social values one can discern among social class groups. (I'll circle back to class as a key best practice in geo-targeting and sequencing distribution gains in Part Four.)

- **Occupational identities:** This is perhaps any adult's primary, *chosen* social identity, and apparently some choose a new one annually. But don't use the taxonomy from your Secretary of State or the US Department of Labor. Have a drink, relax, and imagine occupations in which folks work intensely and daily in highly collaborative teams of 5 to 25 players: pharmaceutical sales reps, nurses, surgeons, etc. These are highly valuable social niches to connect with as an emerging CPG brand—as long as your product line's outcomes are relevant to the group in question. You're looking for occupations that promote tribalistic, collaborative, and emotionally charged work flows. Probably not a market research company or an accounting firm. Just sayin'.

- **Voluntary/recreational identities:** The key here is to select groups in which the outcomes of using your product are relevant to a core activity of the group. If you can also focus on groups that have a continual influx of dabblers, do it. Avoid any recreational groups whose members engage in purely solitary hobbies (i.e., painters, landscape photographers), unless you can find online communities with intense involvement. And your product has to be relevant … still.

Examples of consumer niches with definable CPG product needs include triathletes, ultra-marathon runners, single-track mountain bikers, road racers, new Moms' groups, runners, golfers, Weight Watchers participants, and illness/disease online groups (e.g., diabetes, auto-immune disorders, cancer, etc.), among others. Remember the relevance rule, though. Marketing fancy butt-wipes to the local knitting club makes little intrinsic sense. Marketing them to road cyclists who can't afford to have a painful butt rash on a 100-mile ride is another matter.

As long as using your product is relevant to the group, it doesn't matter which ones you pick. Nor do you have to pick only one. American marketers have an obsessive need to find the single "target consumer" audience. Consumer targeting is not about "The one." You're not writing a romance novel. You're trying to scale exponentially. If two or three awesome consumer niches can generate above-average conversion and excitement early on, then target them all. Invariably, all three love you because your product line fulfills a shared outcome they desire for different reasons. The folks who insist on picking just one target audience are the targeting equivalent of the agency folks who obsess on your "unique selling proposition." These are both unhelpful, limiting beliefs.

You can (and probably should) work with two or three consumer niches to maximize your penetration of local and regional markets. The unifying theory behind your selection should be a common behavioral logic: consumers in these groups will rapidly become heavy-using and, hopefully, vocal fans based on one or more of the product-line's key outcomes. Just select the groups that are the largest locally and present nationwide in top metros. Longboard surfers is probably not that great of a group to assist with a nationwide ramp. Once you've identified the consumer niches that have naturally glommed onto your brand for relevant behavioral reasons (i.e., the love is repeatable in nature), feed them—literally and figuratively—to build strong memorability.

Honor these niches in your consumer outreach. Gratitude is so powerful in building memorability. BigCo cannot credibly show gratitude. Its brands are too big to function like buddies inside social niches. If Brad Pitt walks into your cocktail party, the party will suddenly be about Brad until he leaves, no matter how hard he tries to hide behind the sofa.

Remember what I said in Part One: memorability is the CPG entrepreneur's primary weapon of advantage. Yes, leaning on consumer niches and memorability within them is slower than deploying tons of aggressive, high-impression paid media. But it actually works consistently for low-awareness trademarks with limited distribution—unlike the former BigCo promotional tools. Mass awareness and mass distribution to a mass audience is one model. You simply can't execute it. So, forget about it.

––––––––

The underlying principle making conversion a valuable business goal is the near-term cash value of heavy repeat consumers. However, if you can also learn from their motivations, you should also be able find ways to find more of them. Spending money to stimulate one-time trial or once-a-year trial or twice-a-year trial is simply too risky for a CPG startup or any brand below nine figures in revenue.

Beyond Meat is one brand deliberately building itself purely on light buyers—i.e., buyers with a much, much lower buy rate than the folks who buy beef patties in the meat case. And guess what? They raised a war-chest of capital to take this path toward higher household penetration and scale. This proven (primarily by-BigCo) approach is simply foolish for undercapitalized startups. It's just not even possible.

Yet, you can't just put all your marketing chips into rewarding your high-repeat buyers and hope they'll keep buying more and more and more. If you were selling soda to the living room in the 1960s, this would have been a viable strategy. Today, instead, you have to constantly recruit more heavy users. If you think employees aren't loyal in America today, you should look at Nielsen/IRI panel data on consumer loyalty to CPG brands.

CHAPTER 9

CREATING LIGHT USERS AND CONVERTING THEM

T rial. Repeat. For founders new to CPG, these two words are the most fundamental marketing jargon to burn into your mind if you want to ride the Skate Ramp well and blow past the guys who rapidly got to $5 million on distribution but then slowed to a crawl.

In the CPG industry, trial and repeat are classified as *marketing metrics*. These two concepts have an especially disproportionate role to play in accelerating new premium CPG brands up the Ramp to nine figures. Scaling on one-time trial or two-time trial is a house of cards you do not want to sit on top of. Trust me. When the new entrant suddenly blows in with more money, the trade winds will literally blow you away.

To avoid this, you first need to understand the distinction between *buying* and *consuming*. While it is easy to assume that tracking retail purchases is equivalent to tracking consumer usage, it truly is not. Retail POS purchase-frequency and purchase-volume don't really tell you what's going on during the moment of consumption. This is due to the twin phenomena of volume-based TPRs and multi-pack

UPCs, which encourage high purchase-volumes *regardless* of the actual consumption rate.

For example, I can consume yogurt cups daily but only buy them once every 10 days. I can also consume yogurt cups daily and buy them three or four times a week. Your sales staff can use trade promotion techniques to manipulate purchase volume but not the consumption rate at home.[89]

Time and again, snack and beverage brands (those most likely to generate exponential growth, in general) have used their UPC mix, marketing, and product design to coax consumers from trying to lightly repeating to heavily repeating—in the process generating much of their exponential growth.

They do this by encouraging and nurturing a process of increased usage frequency at the individual level. I call this *conversion*, for poetic reasons. Conversion leads to higher and higher purchase volume and/ or buy rate at local outlets. It drives organic velocity growth entirely from locally available consumer demand. The more an individual consumes a CPG brand, the more likely it is to become habit-forming— basically, a top-choice, if not exclusive, brand on certain eating or drinking occasions.

Your sales team is great, I'm sure, but it cannot generate exponential growth through volume-based TPRs alone. Your TPR lift will quickly hit a wall in a new account and become a poor use of funds that only generate predictable, temporary volume surges at lower gross margins. The deeper the discount (e.g., BOGO), the bigger the temporary, lower profit surge will be.[90] Heroin is not a growth strategy in life or in CPG businesses.

---

89. This is why light buyers and heavy buyers look the same to a near-term focused sales professional. Yet, they're not of the same strategic value in the early part of the Skate Ramp. Besides, less frequent buyers tend not to buy multi-packs for obvious reasons, even if they'll go for a volume-based TPR (e.g., 2/$5).
90. A great, advanced KPI is the non-promoted unit velocity of multi-packs in existing stores. This is a great metric with which to understand if conversion is going on.

So, how do you increase usage frequency?

Finding Frequency Upsides in Your Brand

To increase velocities at existing stores, you need to either increase the consumption rate (and purchase volume) or add individuals in the local shopper base. The latter is easier said than done due to the premium unit-prices of most early stage CPG brands.

Given the power of well-designed premium brands to radically reframe category options, your focus as an undercapitalized founder needs to be on converting consumers to heavy repeat purchase. And it needs to be done before they get distracted by the next new thing to promise similar outcomes (including in unrelated categories).

The primary reason for this is to keep your brand circulating in a residence long enough to generate in-home trial and repeat by other members of the household (i.e., in-home conversion). Although marketers obsess over hip Millennial singles, family households are generally much better initial beachheads for any new brand in CPG. There are more mouths in these homes with the potential to generate steady velocity growth off of your existing base of households in a local area.

When it's time to hit the gas with venture capital, adding households becomes much more critical. Although, as we'll see, this is not simply about adding doors and accounts anywhere and anyhow.

You want to ensure that your heaviest consumption rates at least match those of the category itself locally and nationally. In order to make the conversion process more tangible, let's look at the consumption frequency profile of a real-world, early-stage premium brand selling just under $1 million in trailing annualized sales and operating in just one state.

The diagnosis with Brand Awesome is that it clearly has a problem converting light users to heavier usage. (Figure 18) If that wasn't the case, I would strongly suspect the brand has a problem with targeting and/or availability. It is a common issue for new trademarks of all kinds, but especially those that first created tons of impulse,

Figure 18: Consumer Consumption Frequency Profile for a Premium Brand

Self-Reported Adult Consumption	RTD Beverage Category in the US	Same Category in Home State	Brand Awesome
Sample size	*n=1,500*	*n=1,000*	*n=258*
1x/day or more	31%	28%	~10%
4-6x/week	9%	10%	~8%
2-3x/week	9%	12%	~20%
Once a week	17%	16%	~17%
Less than 1x/week	34%	34%	~45%

Premium Growth Solutions surveys and confirmed repeat buyers of Brand Awesome within the brand's fanbase, June 2019

out-of-home trial and are now trying to gain a foothold in domestic food and beverage consumption.

What should *not* concern you as a founder is something classically trained marketers call *loyalty*. Loyalty is still over-discussed by agencies who like to exaggerate their indirect influence over your consumers' wallets. Anyone who has looked at Nielsen/IRI/SPINS consumer panel data knows how low brand loyalty is on an annualized basis in most value-added categories, especially those with lots of relevant dietary outcomes and innovation. As I discussed earlier, most premium CPG consumers also consume mainstream brands in the same category. (Figure 19) But even the purity freaks aren't brand-loyal within premium, especially if the premium segment is highly evolved with no clear dominant brand (e.g., bars, yogurt, spreads, water, etc.).

Get used to week-to-week disloyalty. Consumers are extremely promiscuous and easily bored. So, the goal of working conversion is not to try to own 100 percent of a consumer's category consumption occasions. Not feasible. Pointless. This is as dreamy as hoping everyone will care about your brand story/mission.

The goal of monitoring conversion is to maximize your formation of consistently heavy users, not just people who occasionally buy a

Figure 19: Other Brands Consumed in the Past 30 Days by Heavy Users of a Local Kombucha Brand

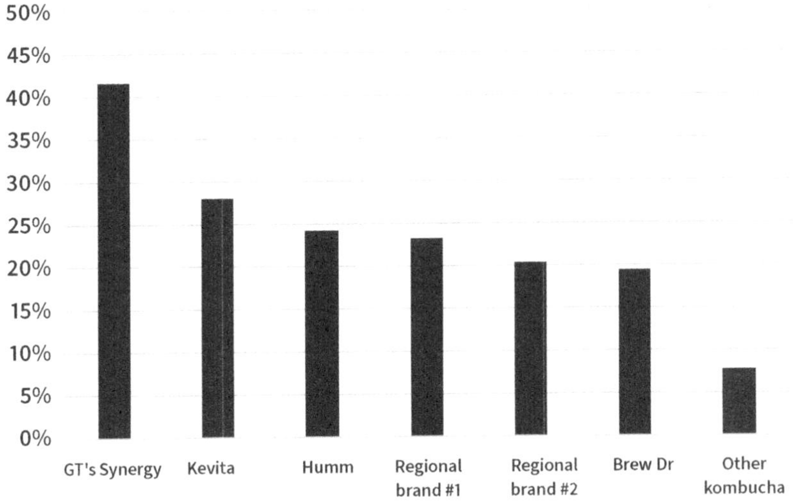

This is a classic example of disloyalty among premium buyers.[91]

ton and consume it slowly. You can determine this is happening when your brand's highest frequency percentages exceed the highest frequency percentages of the category as a whole. (Figures 20 and 21)[91]

As large nine-figure brands, we would expect both La Croix and Kind to have a disproportionate amount of casual, light buyers in their consumer make-up. However, the fact that Kind exceeds the category average in multiple occasions per day while La Croix does not can be seen as an indirect sign of brand health. Kind is moving new consumers through the funnel toward extreme category usage 15 years after launching in the United States. This is the sign of a strong Skate Ramp brand built on velocity growth and consumer pull.

---

91. Premium Growth Solutions client survey, November 2018; n = ~250 heavy users who drink the target brand 1/week or more.

Figure 20: Below-Average Extreme Conversion

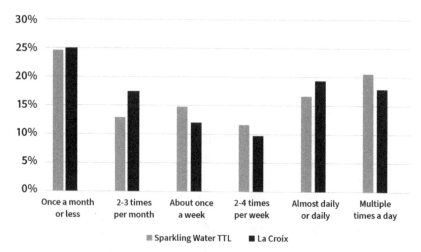

At the time of this survey, La Croix had sub-optimal extreme conversion.[92]

Figure 21: Above-Average Extreme Conversion

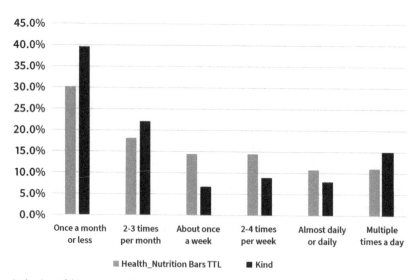

At the time of this survey, Kind was driving above-average extreme conversion.[93]

---

92. Premium Growth Solutions survey, June 2019; n = 1,000 adults.

93. Premium Growth Solutions survey, June 2019; n = 1,000 adults

Skate Ramp Brands Work the Streets

Too many of us remember vitaminwater incorrectly as the meteoric beverage brand that 50 Cent, as its key endorser and investor,
helped launch to stardom in the mid-2000s. That's only true if you are
focused on the journey from $100 million to $350 million in revenue,
acquisition by Coke, yada-yada.[94]

The more critical ramp of 1999–2004, from $0 to $100 million—
before 50 Cent got involved and where I specialize—was much harder
won than some simple celebrity investor/endorser move, signed over
dinner at Spago. Yet, many of us have forgotten all about the real
vitaminwater ramp-up story.[95]

Vitaminwater, and its contemporary, Red Bull, both exemplified
and literally created the modern best practices in grassroots field
marketing. In fact, many of Red Bull's top field marketers went on to
apply their techniques at dozens of other beverage startups. Their
guru, some would say, is Jeff Garrett of the agency Highway 9. Others
would point to Glacéau marketing executive Rohan Oza, the mind
behind vitaminwater's roving fleet of water-tasting vans and brand
hydrologists.

What do I mean by the word *field* in field marketing? Well, the
field consists of any public venue where ordinary consumers gather
for *some purpose other than to try your product* and where your product is astoundingly relevant, hip, cool, legit, whatever generational
adjective you prefer to use.

Due to the gaping mouth of the fee-hungry, middle-market, retail
trade nexus, you've perhaps been pressured into promising to do
store demos at one or more accounts as a condition of getting on the
shelf. This chapter, if it succeeds in nothing else, will hopefully broad-
en your imagination by putting store demos into their proper context.
Perhaps it will inspire you to find ways to negotiate yourself out of
them where they will yield little.

---

94. https://addicted2success.com/motivation/how-50-cent-scored-half-a-billion-dollars/
95. I have nothing against celebrity founders or endorsements, but you can't plan for such a
tactic. Hence, it is largely an irrelevant topic for most CPG founders who don't already have a
celebrity within one degree of separation.

Repeat and the quest for more of it are all about product memorability. Emerging CPG brands have to work 10 times as hard on memorability if they want to accelerate at an above-average rate. Memorability is also what causes repeat to sustain long enough to convert other household members and to drive up purchase volume.

———————

Now, I'm going to take you deeper into the process with which consumers go from trying a premium brand to becoming a stable, repeat buyer for some period of time. More importantly, I'm also going to show you how founders can actually manipulate this process to their advantage using non-traditional persuasive techniques.

Conversion and High-Quality Consumer Trial

The behavioral theory of conversion in premium CPG goes as follows:

. . . Generate high-quality trial among *highly predisposed* consumers,

. . . which leads to high-quality repeat purchase *faster*,

. . . which, in turn, sustains itself *longer at the individual level*,

. . . due to having established *far greater brand memorability*.

Phew! Coffee, anyone? I'm tired just reading this.

One of the most amazing ethnographic research findings from my old days of surfing the pantries of America for Whole Foods, Kraft, Coke, and others is that, during the first months of new premium-brand adoption, consumers often cannot remember your trademark . . . at all. Otherwise gung-ho organic food junkies routinely had to take us to their kitchen and find the package in order to name the brand! Even they were kind of embarrassed about it.

Consumers may buy your trademark four to six times before they remember it. What consumers initially recall are the graphic design elements and product symbolism of the front panel.

The problem is that, when launching, the average premium brand is not doing saturation, high-impression marketing of its trademark to build cognitive receptivity in consumers' minds weeks ahead of it arriving at the shelf. This is a BigCo practice, and even they reserve it for the big launches on their marquee brands.

For a new CPG brand, the consumer's memory of your product experience is doing most of the work. When I say again and again that you must lean hard on memorability as a CPG founder, it's really about leaning on a memorable consumption experience. This experience makes remembering the trademark and package more likely.

The goal of field marketing is to drive accelerated memorability that leads more quickly to high-quality trial than does purely symbolic communications, thereby kicking off the conversion process. Believe it or not, just because the consumer liked your product does not mean they'll buy it ever again. Your tongue, interestingly enough, is not connected to your Cozi, Evernote, or Outlook accounts. For small premium brands, the delay in trademark memorization that I referred to in Chapter 4 also threatens to disrupt the conversion process. This stems from the chaotic shopping routines of modern consumers, who may buy your category at three or four different retailers, of which you are in only one. Argh!

Yet, it is memorability that gets you picked up when they do swing by again to that one channel. Memorability is actually the primary hope you have in overcoming your inevitably spotty local-distribution reach in the early years.

This is where the practice of field marketing comes in. It gives you, the undercapitalized founder, an added tool in driving memorability off of the relatively cheap product samples (i.e., your cost of goods per unit) stacked high in your office. It is unusually efficient in doing one thing that advertising can never do: it allows you to tell your outcome story live in person and then hand the consumer a free chance to perceive it for themselves.

Field marketing taps into a form of cultural rarity that is productive of long-term memorability. That is, calendrically rare public events may happen weekly, at most, but are experienced monthly or less by the average consumer. This lends them a specialness that is conducive to powerful memory formation in a way that doing your laundry twice a week does not. This is because these non-daily social experiences open us up to new information, ideas, and experiences.

Here's a handy list of memory-forming events for budding field marketers to go by:

- **Events with live music.** Huge thronging bass sounds tend to dissolve boundaries between individuals as well as petty notions of personal space. Live music is a social lubricant that opens most folks up to new social signals. The uptight know to stay away.

- **Lifestyle retreats and events,** where extreme idealism is the social lubricant: yoga teacher training, wellness retreats, fitness camps, basically anything on the Left Coast, from San Luis Obispo to Half Moon Bay

- **Resort vacations with family.** Travel opens up most folks to meeting new people and trying new things, including overly "fun" poolside SMORES parties at Westin resorts.

- **Airport nightmares**—delays/cancellations, where shared pain and frustration is the social lubricant between jaded business travelers

- **Standing in public**—interminable lines at Disneyland, the DMV, or Six Flags, where parents especially need to know they're not the only ones about to lose their minds

- **Office parties.** Is there really a need to explain why America's hordes of disengaged employees like an excuse to join in on these? Well, one reason people stay at jobs with task lists that bore them is the friends they have in the office.

- **The first warm day of spring.** This is primordial hominid behavior folks. It dissolves all boundaries of race, caste, and class at least until sunset.

- **Sporting events**—putting 50,000 humans in a building all at once to watch the same 10 to 20 professional athletes do whatever tends to break down social barriers that exist back in your hood . . . plus, the beer

What do all these things have in common? They are social events that remind us we are not alone. They reconnect individuals and families with broader notions of community. In a country where increasingly more individuals live alone and where anxiety disorders are on the rise (as well as self-diagnosed anxiety) and where communal experiences are increasingly virtual, the power of these kinds of moments is only growing for most of us.[96] A neurological shift in our brains literally occurs when we experience these kinds of events. They are the times when culture and chemistry dance together and minds are temporarily susceptible to all manner of influence.[97]

Most importantly, in these kinds of uncommon social settings, humans become open to new sensory and social signals. In fact, many crave them in these settings. They crave interaction. They crave something to drink and eat in the company of others in order to feel less alone.

Plane flight canceled? Let's grab a beer and whine.

Stuck in an endless DMV line? Hey, want some of my Twizzlers? (Yes, guerilla marketing in DMV lines has happened before.)

Did you see that header? Yes! Man, our team is amazing! (Sound of celebratory, stadium lemonade gulping.)

What are you going to do with your yoga teacher certificate? No idea. Let's have some booch across the street and discuss!

Food, beverage, and candy, especially, are critical props in these highly social and memorable moments. Whenever you can sample

---

96. Health and Wellness 2019, a study by The Hartman Group, Inc., found that 63% of American adults were currently treating, or trying to prevent, anxiety and stress, the first time this health concern made it to the #1 spot among many competing health issues.
97. Where *not* to conduct word-of-mouth marketing today? Door-to-door. At your office desk. In a business meeting. These are normative social domains that don't take kindly to interruptions or disruptions from strangers. They don't come up in discussions of word-of-mouth marketing, because they're intuitively the wrong place to conversate about your brand.

your product at these kinds of extraordinary times and do it with meaningful storytelling conversation about its beneficial outcomes, you have the potential to create intense memorability. You are literally having one person tell another one in a high-trust setting (see above list of events that foster social trust) that this thing they're consuming right now will do X for them. They may not believe your product can deliver the promised outcome, or they may not like the taste. But you simply don't have a better opportunity for persuasion than this. A lame demo table at Albertsons is...just...not...the...place.

Event sampling done in the context of real conversations (about the brand or not) is one of the more powerful tools a CPG founder has that does not require a fortune. It is a tool any CPG entrepreneur can utilize, because your unit production costs, even for a premium item are usually somewhere around $1–1.25. A sample given directly by another human being, especially inside an event where a meaningful lifestyle group has gathered, triggers very primordial gift-giving logics in the human mind.

Anthropological research on gift-giving has explored a universal logic across most cultures. That is, recipients of a gift feel obligated to reciprocate to the giver, even if they ultimately reciprocate in a way the giver had not secretly desired (i.e., in your case, immediate and regular purchase). This feeling of reciprocity is most prevalent when the individuals share intense values—hence, the need to sample within values-driven social worlds where you and your team are seen as relevant participants, not pushy impostors.

If the product is well-designed and the outcome story is well-crafted, you have a chance to boost memorability and to hasten the time to creating a repeat purchaser.

Because the live-event sample of a new brand is usually the consumer's first trial, their first real purchase functions as a repeat and not as trial. They will enter the store looking for you, ready to jump-start a habit. The accelerating power of this mindset is worth pausing to consider. For categories consumed daily in the home and purchased at least weekly, trial at a field-marketing event can, and often does, lead to purchase in a matter of hours to days. No one can promise the 98 percent conversion rate that Kind apparently experienced in its early years, but even 50 percent conversion to trial is huge for a small business. In contrast, the time it takes to generate multiple social-media impressions for a retail brand is usually measured in weeks, if not months.

All you have to do is get access to any event with a predisposed subpopulation (discussed in Chapter 8) and hand out samples while you chat them up with your killer outcome story. This story needs to be one-line long, because it's going to come out of your mouth hundreds of times at any event, and more importantly, because you have 30 seconds max to impregnate their memory with your message You should write down your one-liner and keep it with you in an easily retrievable place, like your pocket or smartphone. It should probably be your tag line. Too many premium CPG brands use their tag line to promote their corporate mission, when they should really focus on selling their killer consumer outcome (once they know what it is). Happy repeat consumers will indirectly fulfill your corporate mission.

Conversion versus Trade Techniques as Velocity Drivers

Repeat buyers form the concrete floor of your base business. If their absolute number is not growing, you have a serious challenge ahead, because distribution growth becomes the primary lever. This is not what you want as an undercapitalized CPG company without an experienced national sales team. Only so many new accounts will open every year, anyway (unless you're a cute little unicorn).

The mystery for every young CPG brand is, how long will this awareness-trial-repeat conversion process continue at existing stores?

In my study of the marketing science behind trade promotions, I have never seen any evidence that trade techniques (i.e., features, displays, TPRs) by themselves generate multi-year velocity growth. Rather, these techniques are proven to create permanent baseline lift in new, hip brands and repeatable surges of revenue, much like a year-end salary bonus. But the incremental sales usually don't keep increasing. If you built your revenue on top of frequent promotions, you have generally hurt your profit in order to modestly increase scale.[98]

This kind of trade-promotional lift has a cap on it, since it is based on three factors that are not scalable:

1. The depth of unit discounting. (Only BigCo could really slash ARPs deeply enough to chase huge lift and perhaps survive.)

2. The number of periods you can be on promotion in a year

3. The number of high-visibility placements you will ever be allowed in the store[99]

You know what is more scalable? The number of mouths in the store's trading radius, especially at high-traffic locations.

In kid-heavy suburban zip codes like mine, every transaction is significantly higher and more valuable because the shopper is a proxy shopper for three to five (or more) mouths. If they happen to be zip codes with a large educated population, those folks will be more likely to buy premium CPG brands on a routine basis, potentially in dozens of categories, maybe yours, too.

Visible placements and limited, volume-based TPRs in each store serve to sustain an inflow of new triers. But they are like fuel injectors in your car. The fuel is the consumer. Always. In sustaining velocity growth, what you are trying to do is attract new mouths for years, enticing them to come forward and try the brand as it gains increasingly more memorability and higher instant recall through local social networks (digital and real world).

Same-store velocity growth is not only the master KPI in CPG brand growth; it is also the sign that your conversion funnel is working. If you don't have it, my research suggests that you probably won't

---

98. Michael V. Marn, Eric V. Roegner, and Craig C. Zawada, "The Power of Pricing," McKinsey & Company, 2003.

99. Only Frito-Lay consistently drops dozens and dozens of shipper displays into high-traffic stores on key party weekends (Superbowl, Memorial Day, 4th of July, Labor Day, etc.), an order of magnitude absolutely no one else gets permission to do or could feasibly pull off, anyway.

be riding the Skate Ramp properly. You will be faking it with accreted distribution gains. You may then fall on your ass or simply collapse into a low double-digit, geometric-growth trajectory that you may be happy with, but investors and acquirers may not be.

The Real Power of Sampling

Now that I've explained the math and theory behind the value of conversion, it's time to get more tangible.

When you're a young brand, it's critical to start experimenting with a ground game that primes the conversion funnel and sets it into motion at high-value store locations. This takes time and energy, but it does not require a Series A investment round—at least not in your local market.

Let's snap back to the store demo topic, where I began this chapter. There's one thing about store demos most people fail to grasp in the stress of planning, paying for, and executing them. They introduce your product to non-category buyers.

The traditional assumption most founders make—because most stakeholders in the value chain make it, too—is to assume the premium buyer is coming from within the pool of local category shoppers. If you only appear in a store in your normal category set, this is probably true. But the minute you get secondary placement, shipper displays, and endcaps or you appear in a high-energy store demo, you suddenly get in front of tons of folks who just might be enticed to try the category *right then*. Why? Because of your product symbolism and supreme powers of verbal demo persuasion. And perhaps your stunningly attractive demo staff. Or because, let's face it, you're such a charismatic Insta-founder.

This is precisely why field marketing becomes amazingly powerful outside of the store. With category buyers, you have entrenched brand preferences to deal with. Getting them to pay a price premium in chips may be really hard. Most consumers have a set of brands they purchase each month in value-added categories. They essentially rotate and slosh around inside this set.

If you rely solely on visibility to category buyers at the shelf, you are limiting yourself to a retail buyer's view of the universe and forgetting about the value of your brand's key outcome (which always crosses categories). You are also not following best practices followed by most Skate Ramp brands I've studied. That's because most of them used aggressive field marketing and/or trade placements to get in front of tons of non-category buyers in specific, high-value geographies.

Word-of-Mouth Marketing and Optimizing Conversion

While typically referred to as *field marketing*, nudging consumers into the conversion funnel is better framed as *word-of-mouth marketing* (WOMM). The latter is not—I repeat, *not*—silently handing out samples and ticking boxes at a demo table. (Groan. Sound of head banging on desktop repeatedly.) Word-of-mouth marketing is about engaging in authentic, relevant storytelling about your product experience and its high-value outcomes. If it's flavor, then it's flavor. If it's keeping consumers from gaining five pounds, then that's what it is. Field marketing is intimate and allows you the best possible theater in which to present your product line as a tool to manage the consumer's inner most fears. (See Part One.)

Most of the brands that have been able to create a high-volume conversion funnel have operated in medium- to high-velocity categories, where the package is emptied within a week or less. The reason this is the case is that working out-of-store levers in the neurological context of short-term memory requires that the influenced consumer gets to the store within 72 hours or fewer. If you sit back and think about the worst-case scenario, it should make sense. Imagine trying to get someone to remember your Chicago Marathon finish-line pitch for an awesome low-sugar ketchup (even when accompanied by an awesome fresh hot dog) months later in February, when they finally need a new bottle of ketchup. Not likely.

If, on the other hand, you have something on the order of Red Bull or vitaminwater—something feasibly consumed daily by geeks and that introduces consumers to a new category of offering with new-fangled formulations they're not used to—then you can benefit from locating and nudging optimal consumers into the funnel in a public or lifestyle event setting.

What successful brands have learned is that word-of-mouth marketing only works at all when it literally inserts your brand into extraordinary local moments and settings. It is, ultimately, a geo-targeted field-marketing tool, perhaps the original one before digital marketing overtook the concept. When a brand enters an event and engages the various social networks in attendance, it accesses those local social networks *when consumers are open to sensory influence*—when, in fact, they are actively seeking it out. Not when they are in chore mode, trying to get out as fast as they can (i.e., walking past your supermarket demo table).

The best word-of-mouth marketing, however, is essentially invisible and purely guerilla. Remember the outbreak of weirdos dressed up as Pabst Blue Ribbon bottles, a decade or so ago? Yeah. That was actually part of a massive, national WOMM campaign by an ad agency. I doubt you caught any hint of that, though, because the kids involved did not talk like brand ambassadors. They were smarter than that. They simply had fun talking about PBR to folks who had never had it, many of whom also thought it had gone out of business.

The key to creating high-quality trial, as successful Skate Ramp brands have learned, is to avoid field marketing that is essentially mindless sampling, unless you know you have a product that generates super-high conversion to trial. Instead, you pick relevant events at which to show up, where your product's outcomes make sense. You make your outcome case as poetically and succinctly as possible. Then, you wait ... for trial in the next 72 hours. If store velocities don't show variation, rethink and try again.

PART FOUR
ACCELERATING TO SCALE

PHASE 4 $30–$100M

PHASE 3 $7–$30M

CHAPTER 10

WELL-PACED DISTRIBUTION GAINS

When most early-stage CPG brands decide to accelerate their YoY growth rate, they tend to primarily scale distribution, hoping that more doors will magically lead to proportionately more trial. Doesn't really happen that way. Since it will often take more than six months to figure out what is going on, brokers and distributors will have monetized your business just fine, even if you get delisted eventually. They have a low incentive to tell you, "Hey, look, that's a bad retailer for this kind of innovation and here's why."

In this final section of the book, I want to explore three best practices that force you to accelerate and scale patiently and intelligently along the Ramp. If you follow them, you will avoid fire-hose, non-strategic growth practices that lead to underperformance for premium CPG brands, again and again and again. These key practices also focus your organization on growing velocities as you add doors, the key to staying on the Ramp. I want you to get to nine figures with a business still primed for long-term growth.

So, how do you know if you're ready to accelerate to exponential growth rates (or to maintain them, if you're lucky)?

You're ready to Ramp once you've reached these three broad prerequisites:

1. Made it to Phase 2 (i.e., $1 million trailing, annualized POS sales. No run-rate prayers, folks . . . real trailing revenue.)

2. Understand which attribute-outcome associations will drive moderate to heavy usage.

3. Iterated once or twice to perform well against the three critical KPIs I mentioned in Chapter 5.

Going forward, growth targets should not exceed 200 percent YoY, unless you have solid data (preferably 18 months, at least) suggesting you can exceed this rate and sustain it through organic consumer pull (i.e., not just adding doors). (See Chapter 5.) Even then, I would not plan on this. The larger the trailing 52-week revenue, the harder it is to sustain exponential growth. Imagine driving your car 50 mph and then turning into a headwind; it now takes more gas to maintain your speed than it did prior to the headwind. The headwind only gets worse and worse as you approach $100 million in POS sales. You're not a unicorn.

Maintaining exponential growth in the seven figures is a big challenge. In lower buy-rate categories, national distribution well outside of Whole Foods Market and the natural channel becomes *mandatory*. Companies in these categories end up relying more on distribution to grow quickly. Without significant external funding, you won't be able to launch a promotional effort to increase awareness fast enough to accelerate velocity growth.

However, in categories befitting the Skate Ramp, with offerings well-suited to heavy usage and rapid uptake, the approach to acceleration does *not* lean on ratcheting up wide, omni-channel distribution ASAP.[100] So, when those founders punch it, that is precisely when things get the most dangerous. During Phase 2, retail stakeholders will approach you at this point to serve their own financial interests, especially if you keep showing up at four or five trade shows every year. (You look a little too hungry for sales, my friend.) Saying no to retailers and/or to the overexuberant work of your broker/sales team will become your primary weapon to attain exponential growth that is real, sustainable, and based on growing consumer demand.

It is critical to understand that you can fake the Skate Ramp by adding UPCs or doors . . . for a while. Your velocity trend will eventually give you away, though. (Figure 22)

Figure 22: Faking the Skate Ramp

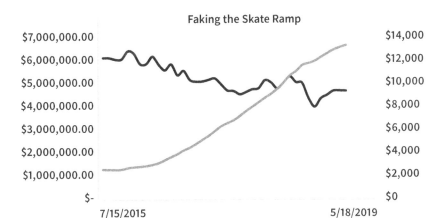

When your velocity trend starts declining, like the premium brand's $/%ACV in this figure, your topline will slow down.[101]

---

100. At this writing, I don't know of any food/beverage businesses that have scaled online to nine figures. In fact, I don't know of any other CPG businesses that have, either. E-commerce is a fantastic launch platform to attain initial seven-figure scale. But, after that, the ability to scale farther appears very limited at this writing. Online, CPG brands end up growing more or less geometrically, not exponentially. The exception may be D2C brands in supplements.
101. AC Nielsen Scantrack, Total U.S., xAOC channels, past four years, quad week ending 5/18/2019.

Would you keep investing in a mutual fund with a steadily declining annual rate of return on principal? Probably not. What Figure 22 shows should terrify you as a founder. If you see something analogous in your own business, you should be unable to sleep . . . for days. I bring this up because velocity decline is amazingly common when premium CPG brands start adding distribution too fast and non-strategically. In fact, you will often see enormous velocity spikes that collapse as initial trial in poorly selected retailers fails to lead to enough repeat (or continued trial).

In this final section of the book, I want to walk you through three key acceleration principles utilized by very successful Skate Ramp brands since the recession:

1. Paced distribution gains
2. Price-pack architecture
3. Class-based geographic expansion

These acceleration principles are a mix of counter-intuitive and basic growth levers in the management of CPG businesses. However, exceedingly few CPG entrepreneurs understand them or are utilizing them at any given moment. It's time to rectify that. All of them focus your business on maximizing or growing velocities—two of them directly, one indirectly.

Calibrating Your Pace of Distribution

Slotting your way around the country will do only so much to scale an emerging CPG business, regardless of how much money you throw at this. Never mind that in the first six months you'll almost always get a sales-lift off of even random trial, unless your product got hidden on the bottom shelf with a black tarp over it. As quick as that initial return on investment (ROI) is, there is no—I repeat, *no*—statistical correlation between absolute gains in %ACV (i.e., breadth of distribution) and average YoY growth for premium CPG brands.[102] Adding

---

102. AC Nielsen ScanTrack, Total U.S., xAOC+C channels, past five years, quad week ending

stores, by itself, does not cause long-term sustainable growth. You are as likely to decline as to grow. Most brokers will never tell you this. Trust me, middlemen have never seen a product line they didn't like or a product that couldn't scale.

Remember, as I mentioned earlier in this book, you will constantly read trade media articles about brands that are launching broadly across all channels or adding thousands and thousands of doors in a single year. These are isolated cases. They are almost all recipients of unusually high amounts of funding you can never plan to receive. What's more, business plans that require ginormous sums of fundraising to accomplish rapid national distribution are fantasies, not intelligent strategies. Prior retailer case studies, more than money, will open future chain doors and on far more favorable terms to you, the undercapitalized founder.

Nothing is more detrimental to properly riding the Skate Ramp then to receive $30–$40 million of capital all at once. Yes, with that much cash, you can "buy" distribution quickly. You can purchase tons of expensive media time. You can hire a huge field sales team before you even know where to deploy them and how.

But you know what you can't buy? Consumer enthusiasm.

And it is consumer enthusiasm that grows velocity at existing points of distribution. Money can only buy indirect influence on this enthusiasm. It cannot create it out of thin air.

In the majority of Skate Ramp cases I've reviewed, the brands in question hit $100 million in xAOC channels with about one-third or less of their total U.S. ACV reach on a quad-week basis. (Figure 23) However, it is increasingly common for velocity of most brands to collapse as distribution breadth ratchets up prematurely. (Figure 24)

Lest you sink into depression upon sight of Figure 24, it should be noted that well-built, innovative brands that grew fast, but patiently and carefully so, along the Ramp can and do generate velocity growth well after maxing out distribution entirely. (Figure 25)

11/21/2015. Analysis courtesy of The Hartman Group, Inc.

Figure 23: Pacing Distribution Growth

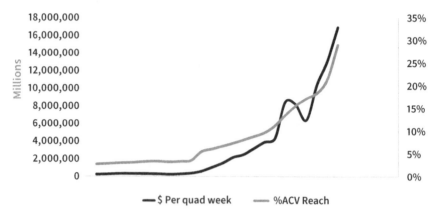

Utilizing around 20 percent of its ACV reach to scale to $100 million left this Skate Ramp brand with the majority of potential distribution as upside for future growth by a strategic acquirer.[103]

Figure 24: Velocity Often Collapses with Overly Rapid Distribution Gains

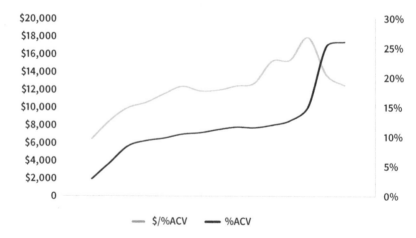

I see escalating distribution alongside tumbling velocity among both unicorns and ordinary early-stage brands, but much less rarely among Skate Ramp brands. This is the inherently greater stability of brands built on steady velocity growth or acceleration.[104]

103. AC Nielsen Scantrack, Total U.S., xAOC channels, past four years, quad week ending 5/18/2019.
104. AC Nielsen Scantrack, Total U.S., xAOC channels, past four years, quad week ending 5/18/2019.

Figure 25: Velocity Growth with Maxed Out Distribution

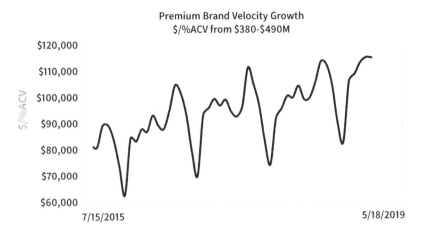

Premium Brand Velocity Growth
$/%ACV from $380-$490M

A leading premium CPG brand continues to grow velocity despite having effectively maxed out distribution in xAOC channels.[105]

The two most powerful near-term sales accelerants in CPG are also the most dangerous if misused by early-stage CPG brands—those are:

- Growing your %ACV distribution
- Lowering your unit price (which tends to happen automatically with rapid omni-channel distribution)

The growth may not last, and it may be followed by rapid decline. Usually, however, it is a significant top-line surge in the short-term for a decent offering. The problem is that surging distribution or lowering price on a trademark with almost no awareness is massively less productive financially than doing either with a brand that has reached $100 million and has broad awareness among predisposed consumers in top markets. Whether or not you ever plan to sell your business, developing a playbook that allows you to pace your use of these two, interrelated mega-accelerants is one of the lesser-known tricks that

---

105. AC Nielsen Scantrack, Total U.S., xAOC channels, past four years, quad week ending 5/18/2019.

Skate Ramp brands have been using since the Great Recession. This strategic restraint ensures that founders (and their investors) build the business on the back of heavy users first, before the time comes to scale well past $100 million via larger and larger quantities of less committed consumers and even purely impulse buyers.

What I just wrote is complete heresy in BigCo, especially on the corporate sales side. That's because contemporary BigCo strategic thinking is biased toward sales and finance techniques. They use the big accelerants from Day 1. They sprint forward to grab hold of some market share and see if they can keep hold of it. That is rarely a successful strategy for them, but it's how their institutions think. They're trapped in a game of grabbing and defending shelf space rather than growing new equities from scratch with patiently aggressive Skate Ramp launches.

Wait. . . . Why on earth would I want to pace my growth after I get to a couple of million in revenue? I've been at this five (or six or seven) years, James. I want my damn reward. I've got investors grooming me for big checks if I can jump to $10 million, quickly. I'm going for it! You can pace yourself to retirement, Professor, thank you very much.

I understand the need for scale. Scale solves most of your financial problems. I get it. By encouraging you to pace your growth (especially in terms of distribution), I am not dictating any particular YoY growth rate other than an exponential one that is not a unicorn rate. In math terms, this ranges from 75 percent to 200 percent YoY growth. That is difficult, but attainable, Skate Ramp growth. According to my research, well over 50 companies have pulled it off since the Great Recession. I'm not asking you to find a black swan.

When I talk about pacing your distribution growth, I'm really talking about three things:

1. Adding accounts (and doors), strategically—where velocities and long-term velocity growth are likely to be strong for years to come. This is an analytical exercise in demand planning that is not at all beyond the budget of a seven-figure company. It's really about setting aside

the time. Most of the relevant data is public. The rest is obtainable from lead buyers and merchandisers, and the better, larger sales brokerages.

2. Making sure to measure velocity trends of new accounts on a quarterly basis, prior to adding more. This is an analytical exercise requiring some fluency in POS data analytics and a budget to obtain access to this information. However, in the absence of POS data, sell-in data trends in high-velocity categories can often tell you a lot.

3. Diagnosing velocity problems and experimenting to solve them, prior to adding big new accounts (500 stores or more) or smaller accounts with high foot traffic in larger, strategically important metros (e.g., Ralph's).

If you are following the lead of successful Skate Ramp brands, you have already optimized your product's attribute-outcome symbolism and sensory experience to scale into an addressable subpopulation of tens of millions of consumers. (That, of course, does not include everyone and certainly not everyone who fills their carts at Walmart.)

Ideally, velocity problems should not be related to your product at this point. They could, however, easily be about product-banner fit or product-geo fit, pricing-banner fit or pricing-geo fit, etc.

If you can keep your suggested retail price (SRP) anchored as high as possible while you grow revenues 100 percent per year and keep %ACV (distribution breadth) relatively low, you will force your team to ensure that you're investing in a playbook that drives same-store velocity growth without using the two over-utilized BigCo accelerants (yet or much at all). The specific mix of moves can and should vary by the offering and the nature of what competitors are doing. However, any playbook to facilitate conversion-driven exponential growth requires that constraints be placed on distribution to force your company into a truly consumer-centric operating culture.

Even if you are well funded at this point, it is unwise for any early-stage brand to mimic the go-to-market or 4P mix of a leading competitor (or "first mover") in the premium space. These are probably nine-figure businesses that have different priorities and options than you. Do something else, something unexpected they won't match. Leaning hard on one tactic done well will pay off better than trying a bit of everything in half-assed, under-resourced executions. This is even true at BigCo, where, believe it or not, most launches have resource challenges, too, unless it's happening under one of the top-selling, highest-margin marks (e.g., Lay's, Oreo, Cheerios, etc.).

Pacing your distribution is about forcing you to let your consumers lead the growth of your business. It forces you to make your conversion funnel work. It forces you to run a B2C business, which will pay huge dividends in terms of staying on the Ramp. It will ensure that your product line is actually becoming a brand and not a specialty commodity (my favorite oxymoron) with no real accumulated brand power.

The 4P acceleration path you ultimately take does not necessarily mandate a rack of expensive agencies, either. The most powerful consumer-demand variable always remains the product experience itself. SkinnyPop and GoGo squeeZ are great examples of lines that used little marketing to accelerate up along the Ramp.

If you're selling *meh* in the mouth, though, your Skate Ramp will be very expensive and highly unlikely to fare well. I have a private list of brands that fell off the Ramp once they got near nine figures because the product was, indeed, *meh*. They skated up the Ramp using paced distribution growth. However, the addressable market for their innovation just wasn't very big once they made it partway up.

The Value in Remaining Under-Distributed During the Ramp Up

If you maintain a restrained distribution pace as you ramp, you will be much more attractive to any potential buyer when your revenues reach mid-eight figures. Why? Every buyer who knows CPG likes to see large distribution upside that they can unlock post-acquisition.

You also will probably stay under the radar for longer, reducing the likelihood of BigCo coming in to outflank you with a flurry of line extensions. This is even more likely if you have anchored your growth in a hard-to-replicate technical process, avoided trade show booths, and not chased every industry PR opportunity for years.

If you need to raise a large Series A or B, you can more realistically promise rapid growth to investors because you have saved the big accelerants for them. How kind of you. Mind you, hitting the gas often means maintaining 75 percent to 100 percent YoY growth—which, I can assure you, is really, really hard after roughly $25 million in sales. Most early-stage premium brands average out at 30 percent YoY growth as they hit $100 million in trailing POS sales (around $40–$50 million on their books).[106] If the rest of your business is above average in design and performance, you can beat these odds and remain under-distributed.

A Short Detour on the Walmart Trap for New Premium Brands

Chasing high-volume chain sales via, say, select Walmart locations presents a clear and present danger to a young, vulnerable premium CPG brand. It requires much lower unit pricing to generate volume sales, because Walmart and other everyday low-price (EDLP) grocers utilize locally low unit price-points in almost every category to attract shoppers. (EDLP supermarkets will force heavy trade-discount promotions as part of their overall retail share of wallet strategy.) Discount retailers like these basically bank on large volume to make up for their attractive lower prices. Walmart had this down to a science…before Amazon, ALDI, and dollar stores. It's in Walmart's DNA to suck your unit pricing down-market, because their shoppers tend to respond to this, historically.

While I occasionally meet an entrepreneur that has been allowed into Walmart at a Whole Foods price point, it is usually an illusion.

---

106. AC Nielsen Scantrack, Total U.S., xAOC channels, quad week ending 12/31/2016; n = 1,600 food/beverage brands selling $1–$100 million from 2013-2016. Analysis courtesy of The Hartman Group, Inc.

Even if the price point stays, the trade-off will be in unit velocities, especially when you are surrounded by vastly cheaper alternatives in such an EDLP retailer. Being in 4,500 stores can produce a lot of volume very quickly. However, when you find out the U/S/W average for your brand is far below a competitor's (or your own) at Kroger or Whole Foods, you will then understand why going down-market too early is a money-losing, strategic face-plant in most cases. If you have a unicorn with unicorn velocities in local supermarkets, then you can probably pull it off. But for most new and young CPG brands, going into Walmart super early while still anchoring your SRP high is unlikely to generate a business with sustainable sales growth.

Even brands that generate stable velocities at Walmart will often literally run out of shoppers to convert very quickly, leading to a stunning reality: low to no growth in the world's largest retailer. Adding a couple million of sales revenue in a year is exciting, until ... it ... just ... won't ... grow ... after that. Don't plan on being the exception. This problem is even more likely if you bring something leading edge into Walmart.[107]

There are several reasons you might run out of shoppers quickly at an EDLP retailer, like Walmart. A premium price point is the number-one reason. The second most common reason is that shoppers cannot even notice you, because you will never, ever get a Walmart endcap. Those are reserved for predictable, volume-moving trademarks, including their store brand Great Value, and they are not for rent. The third biggest reason is because the average category shopper has zero interest in your premium attributes (i.e., habitual comfort in their usual brands and attributes).

Aside from disappointing velocity trends, heading down-market to EDLP retailers too early also sabotages your pricing power in the eyes of consumers and retail trade stakeholders. You can easily accelerate the commoditization of your emerging brand before it has even moved the beyond its training pants.

---

107. Even Walmart is currently open to running "tests" in 100–400 stores prior to rolling new brands out farther.

Given that about 40 percent of Whole Foods shoppers also shop at Walmart, being on Walmart shelves exposes your brand to massive image confusion.[108] If they discover you at Walmart, some very high-value consumers will subconsciously devalue you as some kind of cheap fraud, a company trying to pull something over on them. I've heard this accusation so many times from upmarket consumers (who buy lots of premium products), my ears ache.

———————

Pacing distribution requires an extremely data-driven, analytic, and strategic sales leader. These folks exist but are hard to find. Your ability to pace distribution will also depend on your ability as a founder to say no to your sales team, effectively and without demoralizing them. This is why I push annual strategic plans that get everyone on the same page and force everyone to utilize the same criteria to measure the success of their specific functional efforts. This is much easier in a small company than in BigCo, where I have seen truly sad, sh$t-show, turf wars that make high school cliques look like kindergarten circle-time spats. If you want to pace distribution growth as slowly and carefully as I'm recommending, pick your sales leader carefully. The average CPG sales professional will burn this book as the heresy it truly is.

———————

108. Food Shopping in America 2017, The Harman Group, Inc.; n = 2,004.

CHAPTER 11

PRICE-PACK ARCHITECTURE

n the previous chapter, I discussed your distribution breadth (and the related reduction in average unit pricing that omni-channel distribution tends to force) as a prime CPG accelerant to deploy very carefully. In this chapter, I'm going to address a much under-discussed second accelerant for early-stage CPG companies that creates intense surges in velocity. It is not a dangerous accelerant and should be utilized as soon as possible.

BigCo calls this growth accelerant *price-pack architecture.*

Say what?

Yeah, I know. More BigCo fancy talk. But, trust me, you do want to suffer past it, because price-pack architecture is the most strategically intelligent way to both reduce ARP (i.e., relax your effective per-pack pricing to the consumer) and efficiently accelerate volume in existing core markets.

Indeed, smart founders have cleverly used price-pack architecture to accelerate while watching others in the rear-view mirror limping along toward $25 million in POS sales, at best.

For a BigCo brand like Lay's or Coke, price-pack architecture involves major internal specialization. It is a well-honed science that is tightly linked to world-class behavioral research on real-world consumption. The two variables involved are simple enough: pack size (i.e., ounces) and unit SRP. The "architecture" is created by designing and distributing multiple pack-sizes at specific, unique price points in order to maximize relevance to differently sized consumer audiences and, more importantly, differently structured consumption occasions, with different consumption volumes. (Remember the occasion bit. I'm going to circle back to that, soon.)

As pack size goes up, the price per ounce typically goes down, giving the consumer what is known in the industry as a *built-in discount*. However, to obtain this clever discount, the consumer actually has to pay you more money. Yum! They have to buy a higher standard retail price (SRP) per UPC. You get more money per sale. They get the perception of a great deal. You, the founder, get a whole lot more than a boost in cash flow (as I'll explain in a bit).

The Evolution of Price-Pack Architecture

The early leaders in price-pack architecture were the big soda companies. To be honest, these guys are like the NASA (or SpaceX) of CPG. They always have been. By 1949, Coca-Cola was managing the following price-pack architecture in retail grocers for GI Bill America.

- 1 glass bottle (6.5 oz) went for a nickel. (This was the more or less fixed price for all individual bottles of soda in the United States.)
- 6-pack for 25 cents, a built-in discount of 5 cents
- 24-pack for 1 dollar, a built-in discount of 20 cents[109]

However, if you talk to anyone over the age of 75 (I've spoken to dozens and dozens in my career), they will tell you that soda drinking in the 1940 and 1950s was culturally framed as a "treat." It was not a go-to beverage akin to water, like it still is for millions of Americans today. People did not down bottle after bottle on the couch while Jackie Gleason crooned on their tiny, grainy, black-and-white TV screens. We were also a hell of lot thinner back then, too, if you look

---

109. http://www.foodtimeline.org/foodfaq5.html

at your own family photos (and thank Kodak for those memories). Multi-packs of soda sold in the 1940s went almost entirely to parties and events, not to solitary couch-surfers.

By the 1960s, post-World War II American suburbia was a fully realized addition to the history of human settlement patterns. Leisure time was way up. Work hours had gone way down across all social classes.[110] The timing was ripe for soda brands to conquer the home, because more time at home meant more instances of "thirst" would occur there. Replacing coffee and water was the implicit, if not explicit, goal. The soda companies of that era did an amazing job over several decades, especially with the help of their diet marks. Price-pack architecture was key to this corn-syrupy conquest.

In the late 1960s, Pepsi used clever market listening to sense the huge untapped home soda opportunity and then designed technology to make it work in the supply chain. Enter our young, dashing hero: John Sculley. Yes, that John Sculley, more famous as the doomed CEO of Apple Computer. Sculley and his team noticed that no matter how many bottles they sold into American homes, the soda would get consumed and replenished on the exact same purchase cycle. Purchase cycle = stable. Purchase volume = not maxed out yet. The consumer was leading this soda revolution, and it was definitely not being televised.

As much as PepsiCo would like to claim it in 2019, they did not invent the two-liter soda bottle in 1970 as a loyalty reward for heavy drinkers. (The two-liter arrived on the scene way before such thinking existed among consumer-brand executives.)[111] Rather, it was literally a cheaper way for Pepsi's supply chain to move larger and larger volumes of soda into the consumer's apparently ever-thirstier homes. Six-packs of glass bottles delivered only 39 ounces. Two-liter plastic bottles deliver 68 ounces at a time! The same logic sends railcars, rather than dump trucks, full of coal to coal plants. It was also the only

110. https://scholar.princeton.edu/maguiar/publications/measuring-trends-leisure-allocation-time-over-five-decades and https://ourworldindata.org/working-hours
111. John Sculley, *Moonshot! Game-Changing Strategies to Build Billion-Dollar Businesses* (Rosetta Books, 2014).

way Pepsi could ensure retailer acceptance of increased retail soda volumes at a time when organic growth in at-home consumption was causing a near constant headache of broken glass bottles for chain retailers. (Yes, the manufacturer always took the blame for retail floor mistakes back then, too. Good grief.)

The two-liter was invented to move as much volume as possible onto at-home, casual drinking occasions and casual at-home parties, two types of occasions where large quantities of soda were (and are) rapidly consumed. Chug-a-lug. Glug. Burp. The principle behind offering large pack sizes in a CPG category is, as I said earlier, super simple. Offer the consumer a per-ounce price discount buried within a higher SRP item that dramatically increases your volumes. But something else magical happens, too. Large pack sizes cleverly encourage daily brand engagement and boost memorability inside the home. The larger package is literally a larger billboard. Over time, these large packs help the brand become like a favorite T-shirt or pair of shoes.

Don't believe me? I had a high school friend in the 1980s whose mom lined the right side of the family garage with 10 to 20 two-liter soda bottles at any given time. (Believe it or not, her children were underweight!) It was her back-inventory room. Every time they pulled into the garage, the brand(s) got free ad impressions.

As the distant second-tier soda player in 1970, Pepsi needed some magic in order to ramp up, and the two-liter was key for them. It was an industry game-changer. Coke was caught flat-footed.

If we put on our anthropology caps now, we can see that the two-liter bottle removed the physical and social annoyance of opening 6 to 12 cans or bottles at home. It also eliminated the occasion-based price premium those pack sizes had always commanded. The at-home soda occasion was too ordinary to merit paying a convenience store or vending-machine premium that had built the major soda brands. The two-liter innovation was a major business coup for Pepsi and serves as a classic example of price-pack architecture at work, growing volumes by fashioning the right price-pack combination for strategic, high-volume potential households.

Today, as then, CPG businesses get more profitable with increased volumes, because the cost of goods and go-to-market costs come down on a per-ounce basis. The brilliance of price-pack architecture is that it is a win-win for the consumer and the company—profitably scaling volume while avoiding the gross profit damage caused by excessive temporary price reductions (TPRs). Multi-packs, specifically, also grow same-store velocities at the unit level (versus the UPC level). *Ka-ching!*

Skate Ramp Brands Do Price-Pack Architecture

There is a behavioral logic to price-pack architecture that founders should understand, because other premium CPG entrepreneurs have used it to ride the Skate Ramp, brilliantly. Offering multiple pack sizes allows you to extend your brand onto incremental occasions or simply to maximize at-home velocities. Price-pack architecture may, or may not, increase your per-account velocities at every account, but it will accelerate $/%ACV velocities in a national business.

SkinnyPop is a premium brand that did this wonderfully when it extended into Costco in 2012[112] via potato-sack size bags my nine-year-old could sleep in. Apparently, there is a need for this pack size, folks. I had no earthly idea. The brand also launched twin-packs and single serves relatively early on. (Figure 26)

Movie theaters established the precedent for mass popcorn inhalation in the 1980s. Yet, these buckets of joy are filled with more butter than a wedding cake and consumed only at a theatre, where the low light conceals our abominable, filthy sinning. Sort of.

Ready-to-eat (RTE) popcorn was already growing fast prior to SkinnyPop's emergence, but there was a problem. At home, the lights are on, and you couldn't so easily rationalize your emptying of a Popcorn Indiana movie-theater flavor bag on a random Tuesday evening (without the movie). The buy rate of RTE popcorn was OK, but not like potato chips, because, prior to SkinnyPop's launch, this stuff was coated in fat or sugar, grease, and all manner of naughtiness. Skinny-

---

112. This is the earliest web reference to SkinnyPop's presence in Costco.

Figure 26: Example of Skate Ramp Brand Pack-Size Variation

Note: This is the current 2019 pack array for Skinnypop. Images courtesy of Amplify Snack Brands, Inc.

Pop was the first RTE popcorn brand to let us pound the popcorn at home any day of the week with none of the aching regret that comes with pounding a bag of kettle-corn or movie-theater popcorn. Gross. I think I'm going to be sick. Excuse me.

Perhaps the true master of contemporary price-pack architecture—the example to follow in medium- to high-velocity categories—is Kind bar. When my old team at The Hartman Group looked at what was responsible for the phenomenally exponential topline acceleration of this brand, we discovered that it was almost entirely due to launching a plethora of pack sizes aimed at increasingly heavier, quasi-religious, consumption frequencies.

When we looked at the data in 2016, we saw the following retail pack sizes for sale: one-count, four-count, five-count, twelve-count, and eighteen-count. Kind bar even took price-pack architecture to its modern extreme with its ahead-of-the-curve, online D2C Kind Advantage program. This club still offers the strongest per-bar discount you'll find across the brand franchise, as long as you're willing to purchase box loads. (I'm sure they'd give you a pallet discount, if you came to the manufacturing facility with your own truck.) Almost all of their D2C boxes of bars sell for less than $1 per bar—with free shipping—when you purchase 20 or 40 at a time. Whereas, most in-store Kind bar deals bottom out at 10 bars for $10.

I'm not making pricing recommendations for your brand here. I'm just showing how elaborate price-pack architecture can get for one brand and one product form. I mean, really, how many drizzled trail-mix rectangles can one person eat? Apparently, a sh*t ton.

The Magic of Increasing Usage Occasions

I've talked about the consumer and company benefits of built-in volume discounts for multi-packs and how they can cause same store velocities to surge exponentially like no trade promo program your broker has in his toolbox.

To make use of this powerful tool, though, founders need to tweak one of the rules of premium growth discussed in Chapter 7: relaxing per-unit pricing. When multi-pack UPCs get introduced, your brand-level ARP will actually start growing, not declining (unless you get fancy pants like BigCo and use ounce-equivalized unit pricing—ooh, fancy). For example, adding multi-packs increased the per-unit average retail price (ARP) for the following premium CPG brands over a five-year period:

Salty Snack Brand A	from $3.51/unit to $3.75/unit[113] (ARP increase)
Bar Brand A	from $1.80/unit to $2.68/unit[114] (ARP increase)
Water Brand A	from $1.61/unit to $2.69/unit[115] (ARP increase)

Likewise, in Chapter 8, I delved into the power of leveraging multiple niche consumer audiences together as word-of-mouth and velocity accelerants. Price-pack architecture, however, is built on a slightly different targeting variable: *consumption occasions*. Occasions are the variable of variables in CPG growth strategy (especially food and bev-

113. AC Nielsen Scantrack, Total U.S., xAOC+C channels, past five years, quad week ending 11/21/15. Analysis courtesy of The Hartman Group, Inc.
114. AC Nielsen Scantrack, Total U.S., xAOC+C channels, past five years, quad week ending 11/21/15. Analysis courtesy of The Hartman Group, Inc.
115. AC Nielsen Scantrack, Total U.S., xAOC channels, past five years quad week ending 5/18/2019. Premium Growth Solutions analysis.

erage). The concept of consumption occasions is built on a simple formula directly related to purchased volume: number of people × amount consumed by each × frequency of this occasion per week (or month).

One of the worst things a founder can do is to distribute a product nationally that gets primarily consumed *episodically*, like once a month or less. If your heaviest repeat buyer is infrequent, you will have a problem riding the Skate Ramp. You soon will be tempted to chase doors, rather than focusing on what should be your prime objective— velocity growth.

This is made only worse if your product is sold in a shelf set where most brands are consumed daily or at least weekly. That means the consumer is buying both you and other brands in the set, but the more frequently purchased brands have significantly greater memorability by sheer force of "advertising" impressions in the pantry and fridge and via "time in hand." You will have become forever a special-occasion brand. And your special occasion-ness will grow stronger over time, until you've trained tens of thousands of consumers to see you only as a once-a-month indulgence. I call it the *fancy jam trap*.

Fancy does not create scale, folks. Because "fancy" screams "niche occasions" that . . . just . . . never . . . happen. The only way to scale such a CPG brand is to capture a very large percentage of these infrequent occasions. That requires rapid, expensive, national distribution surges well ahead of the ability of a new trademark to generate awareness. The only way to pull it off successfully would be to have an enormous marketing budget in too many markets at once. Even then, it's not at all clear that a scalable buy rate is even there without slashing your unit pricing.

I'll be honest, sometimes the category is simply framed as a special occasion one in food culture. These kinds of categories just can't ride the Skate Ramp, no matter what you do. To win, you have to design something like BarkThins that reframes the relevant occasions for the larger category (e.g., chocolate). The entire business strategy has to be built around this.[116]

Price-pack architecture is about catering to different occasions having a relative frequency that generates differing consumption rates. Smart, informal consumer research with your fans can help you determine whether they are quietly going out of stock at home without telling you. This is a sign that you've entered ordinary consumption occasions that occur daily in the consumer's life. You've hit gold for premium brands. It means you will start taking market share from large market-share leaders who are too big to care about you . . . yet.

Having price-pack architecture in place as you accelerate also allows you to migrate consumers toward higher-volume, higher-SRP units over time as they convert into geeks. You are essentially preventing the final frontier of out-of-stocks: the home. A deepening consumer habit, therefore, is velocity growth over time. Out of respect, I'll call it the *Law of Sculley*.

———

This is a perfect point at which to summarize my thoughts on velocity growth, which have been slowly accumulating throughout the book. Folks who manage velocity growth in a disciplined fashion conduct these phases in the following order of priority on a per-door basis.

Phase 1   Increase visibility/discoverability in store.
Phase 2   Increase household penetration locally.
Phase 3   Increase the individual consumption rate by adding occasions for consumption.

Most founders understand the first phase of velocity growth. Few understand the last two—both of which are critical to riding the Skate Ramp. Many of the top performers accomplished this, some without really doing it deliberately.

———

116. Two brands have pulled this off before. BarkThins quickly built a premium dark-chocolate brand by going to market as an everyday, munchy snack. SkinnyPop took RTE popcorn and liberated it from the Q4 kettle-corn tin trap, a more generalizable example of reframing a category's dominant occasion structure.

Yet, I wouldn't rely on SkinnyPop luck myself. Price-pack architecture is something most seven-figure CPG brands can plan and start to deploy early on the Ramp, especially in food. It can be a very wise justification for a capital raise, as long your investors understand this seldom-discussed second accelerant's long-term, brand-building power.

The more you master this three-phased velocity acceleration approach, the easier it will be to stay on the Skate Ramp through $100 million and beyond (assuming you're not selling fermented kale juice) and to do it without squandering %ACV upside. That was *not* a green light to develop fermented kale juice. Please don't.

CHAPTER 12

CLASS-BASED GEOGRAPHIC EXPANSION

I n premium CPG, the commonly given advice is to start in the natural or specialty channels, prove yourself, and then use conventional channels to scale the business. Yawn. How quaint. So 2005.

One of the great ironies of premium CPG can be observed at the major trade shows for natural and specialty products, where companies exhibiting there today have started online, in fitness retail, in office cafeterias, in coffee shops, and/or even in your local Safeway. Chobani, in my opinion, was the real wake-up call to industry leaders. It launched in quite ordinary New York and Pennsylvania supermarkets (e.g., Shoprite) and produced phenomenal velocities right out of the gate.[117] You don't need to start at Whole Foods to win anymore. Today, the major trade shows are increasingly full of buyers from Kroger, Safeway/Albertsons, Ahold, Walmart, Target, etc. I will not be surprised if I see a Lidl, ALDI, or Family Dollar name tag very soon. I'm looking, believe me.

---

117. https://hbr.org/2013/10/chobanis-founder-on-growing-a-start-up-without-outside-investors

Despite the upending of the traditional channel sequencing for premium CPG, I have seen no evidence that one fundamental go-to-market principle has weakened in power: class-based geographic expansion.

Premium CPG innovations scale most reliably and efficiently when they first enter retail environments with strong premium merchandising commitments[118] in upmarket zip codes and then sequentially enter more middle-market zip codes. This is essentially what I call *class-based geographic sequencing of distribution.*

Not only does class divide American society, it divides most major supermarket chains, as well. In the United States, supermarkets are neighborhood grocers at their core. They have always adapted to neighborhood demand or gone quickly out of business. Really quickly.

While it is not a polite conversation topic, Americans live in highly class-based neighborhoods (i.e., zip codes). If this has not yet dawned on you, then spend some time on Zillow.

So, why is this admittedly obnoxious truth relevant to your acceleration planning and to your journey along the Skate Ramp?

Because educated, high-earning, professional households (roughly 10 percent of the U.S. population,[119] depending on how you define it) live in upmarket geos. These folks support your high unit prices early on. That allows a line to scale initial volumes ($10–$25 million) with fewer buyers *and* without needing to resort to excessive trade discounts just to convince the less motivated to try it.

This sociological master strategy leverages the behavioral phenomenon of purchasing select premium goods as hyper-modern identity markers; it leans heavily on status buyers. I talked about the status buyer in an earlier chapter. Educated elites in the United States gravitate to this behavior in increasing numbers, largely because they have abandoned the traditional social values of pre-World War II America.

---

118. Snagging 30–50% of non-season end-cap displays is a great indicator of strong premium merchandising commitments, in my experience.
119. At The Hartman Group, my team used raw US Census data to calculate the percentage of Americans with a bachelor's degree living in a household with at least $100,000 in annual income a few years ago.

They actively seek to delink from inherited social traditions (and inherited brands as well).

They also subconsciously gravitate to high unit pricing in ordinary consumer items as an implicit social differentiator. You can come to this conclusion on your own in their homes, next time you show up. As a test, try this line of inquiry: When you see a premium brand, ask them why they consume it. Initially, they'll give you a pat, surface answer having something to do with being healthy or having an awesome taste, because it's easy and polite. Continue to ask why. Keep needling like an annoying toddler until they get frustrated and blurt out something along the lines of, "Because I don't want to drink crap," or "Look, it's not 1985 anymore, OK?"

Those needled utterances are deeply subconscious, class-affinity statements connected to a desire to be seen as hyper-modern and not as a cultural traditionalist. (This is not exactly the same as being a Democrat. Just saying.) It can take a while to get the confession. They probably won't realize they just came off as snobby. Because well-educated people are trained not to appear obnoxious about class hierarchy, they tend not to believe these forces affect their behavior. That's why you won't often find these confessions in open-ended survey responses.

I am not saying that these high-falutin folks don't buy Doritos or Dr. Pepper. Not at all. They surely do. Just like lots of married men who love their wives sneak in some porn viewing once in a while. Gasp! And why a vegan once confessed to me in a research interview that she had to hit McDonald's once a month to indulge in a nostalgic Big Mac. Well, well. Remember: the purity buyers I mentioned in Chapter 8 are almost impossible to measure in databases. That's how rare they are.

Similarly, upmarket status buyers that can quickly launch premium CPG businesses are very selective with their packaged goods purchases. This is why their premium brand purchasing frequently skews to categories on public display (items shared in the home at BBQs, items taken to the office, consumed in public, showcased at Q4 dinner parties, etc.). Think Voss water bottles. Enough said.

This small group of elite Americans is also more likely to include highly networked social circles of friends, who applaud and expect lots of premium buying (whether for surface-level health or culinary reasons), even if it's in a select group of CPG categories. They can accelerate awareness of your brand very quickly via word-of-mouth.

These consumers also tend to live near each other, because class has become the fundamental social baseline driving neighborhood dynamics. This is especially so now that ethnicity and one's extended family have been more or less obliterated as residential principles for the middle and upper-middle classes.

The Power of Upmarket Geos

You may not agree with my depiction of the social-class politics of premium consumer goods. I accept that. However, indulge me as I explore the practice of launching in upmarket geos and its value to your premium CPG business.

Launching in select upmarket geos is a proven growth model that Skate Ramp brands have used to spread from predominately elite to predominately middle-class zip codes, while simultaneously supporting their pricing power, cash flow, and gross profitability. Class-based geographic expansion also paces distribution such that less sophisticated consumers have sufficient time to familiarize themselves with new modern attributes and foodways. A slower, more intelligent geographic spread down-market allows premium brands to culturally prepare and influence the broader, Walmart shopper base ahead of time. It literally primes down-market consumers so they are ready and waiting for your offering once it's time to get there (i.e., when you can relax the pricing to barely above category unit averages).

Upmarket geos are full of college-educated and middle- to upper-income households. The level and kind of education is more predictive of a hyper-modern diet than mere income. Where families are present in these zip codes, premium CPG spending can be very high per trip, as well.

Today, there are roughly 34 metropolitan areas in the United States where 30 percent or more of the adult population (25+ years) has attained a bachelor's degree or higher.[120] While this is only 3.65 percent of all major cities in the United States, it does represent 64 million adults. We live in an era essentially dominated by educated elites.

The largest American cities are all located within these 34 metro areas. That's because the country's largest cities got that way because a college-educated elite built and still controls the primary commercial institutions that have made each of those cities into the metropoles they are today.

However, when you drill down within these 34 metropoles to the county, zip code, and census tract/neighborhood levels, the educational attainment apartheid becomes more severe as the geographic area becomes smaller. So, a specific subset of neighborhoods within these 34 metro areas serve as the key upmarket-launch geos for premium CPG goods.

One premium-focused retailer that literally built most of its approximately $15 billion empire inside such upmarket geos is Whole Foods Market. In the 1990s and early 2000s, this now famous chain accelerated by building and buying retail stores in college/university towns across the United States. They even bought out local health-food chains to gain access to those geos. This is why Whole Foods has some curiously old stores in the Midwest, where many East and West Coasters might assume WFM must surely be a cultural newcomer.

Why did WFM do this? Because college/university towns are heavily populated with a combination of young, college-educated adults; post-grad-educated adults; and young families in tight social networks of professors, students, and support staff. These idealistic social worlds are highly conducive to rapid premium adoption across CPG categories. They are enthusiastic zones of applause for bold dietary alterations. They are factories of class mobility from the middle to

---

120. The 34 U.S. metro areas are: Washington D.C., San Jose, San Francisco, Boston, Raleigh, Austin, Denver, Seattle, Minneapolis, New York City, Baltimore, Hartford, Portland (Oregon), San Diego, Atlanta, Chicago, Philadelphia, Kansas City, Columbus, Richmond, Milwaukee, Dallas, Nashville, Charlotte, St. Louis, Los Angeles, Pittsburgh, Salt Lake City, Indianapolis, Sacramento, Cincinnati, Houston, Buffalo, Providence.

the upper-middle classes, as well. College is a time in life when a large number of young adults make huge dietary shifts and are very impressionable to premium marketing and premium influences. They are also forming long-term class aspirations and goals. Whole Foods was super smart. You can call the company *elitist*, if you like, but the strategy works. In its early years, these geos also provided Whole Foods with a large, local supply of amazingly well-educated, well-spoken retail associates.

My experience on the ground is that, in geos where that kind of heavy social support for premium buying exists, premium sales tend to explode per-capita. When the geo is also a state capitol, like Madison, Wisconsin, you also have a self-contained laboratory for early experimentation with broader, less sophisticated, and less culturally demanding middle classes (i.e., the average state government worker).

Today, Hollywood has largely teamed up, officially and unofficially, with elite consumers in these geos to help accelerate trends faster and faster. America's upper-middle class is the portion of America that has birthed virtually all of the major food trends in the past half century.

Here's another, much less controversial way to look at it: You need to launch and experiment within the social worlds where premium CPG trial is the easiest, where there is the least resistance. That gives your product memorability a chance to generate high-velocity sales per store without over-discounting, so you can gain initial traction.

Since memorability is the fundamental competitive weapon of the undercapitalized entrepreneur, *where* you seek to become memorable early on and *how* you geographically spread your memorability are crucial variables in any successful acceleration plan. Grow velocity in geographic areas where large numbers of consumers are likely to remember and latch on to your product and share it within their social circles. Don't waste your resources trying to ramp in sparsely populated geos where the tiny few who like your product and find it memorable simply don't have enough other people around them to influence. Reach out to those geos last. If you've ever been to a health food store in a rural county, you know what I'm describing. The regulars at these stores are alienated folks, and it doesn't take long to un-cover this alienation over a cup of coffee at the local diner. "Oh, Sally? Yeah, she sure is a bit kooky . . ."

Siggi's is one of the more recent Skate Ramp victors who followed the proven path from upmarket geo to mid-market geo. They started in Whole Foods and spread nationally there before entering conven-tional supermarkets. At the time they launched in Manhattan, this was the only path available in terms of channel sequencing, due to their $2.79 per unit starting price point (or $3.55 in 2019 dollars). From there, the brand went into select Safeway/Albertsons and Kroger stores, but remained out of Walmart and EDLP grocery stores prior to reaching $100 million in sales.[121]

The traditional channel sequencing during siggi's acceleration just happened to mirror a class-based expansion at the zip-code level. It took place in such a way that the brand maintained high average-unit pricing as it scaled. Siggi's skyr launched in 2006 at $2.79 per cup, stayed above $2 per unit through 2011, and then started exploding exponentially at $1.78 per unit in 2015, the beginning of its ramp to glory.[122] Among other things, this allowed the brand the gross profit flow to avoid large amounts of institutional capital that tends to lead to overly hasty attempts to ride the Ramp.

Omni-Channel Shopping Among Upmarket Shoppers

As I mentioned in Chapter 8, Whole Foods Market shoppers typically do not get most or all of their groceries at WFM each month. In fact, less than 2 percent of U.S. adults are doing this.

If we look at cross-channel shopping behavior anchored from the perspective of past thirty-day WFM shoppers, we see that major, na-tional retail-chain networks overlap substantially with this specialty retailer's shopper base. In fact, most of the national banners with the

---

121. Internet research conducted in 2016; courtesy of The Hartman Group, Inc.
122. Time-stamped internet research for the respective years; Premium Growth Solutions, June 2019.

highest degree of overlap with WFM are those that also have significant store presence in upmarket geos[123] and, consequently, have an upmarket skew to their general shopper population.[124]

For example, more than a third of grocery buyers who report shopping at Whole Foods Market in the past 30 days also report purchasing groceries at the following retailers in the past 30 days:[125]

Walmart Supercenters	38 percent
Costco	38 percent
Target	35 percent
Kroger	35 percent
Safeway/Albertsons	32 percent

This cross-channel shopping among Whole Foods shoppers might suggest that, if you want to reach upmarket shoppers, hell, almost any point of distribution is a good one, even Walmart. At the brand level, however, this kind of cross-shopping behavior can be deceptively inviting to your sales team and potentially deadly to growth.

Whole Foods has seen Kroger as their Enemy #1 ever since I was a consultant for them in the early 2000s, because WFM's shopper base and Kroger's overlaps so much in specific high-value WFM zip codes. The more common behavior of premium shoppers is still to obtain perimeter fresh items and end-cap impulse items from Whole Foods and then buy most other groceries (i.e., packaged food and beverages) at a local supermarket or Costco.

But now a substantial portion of Whole Foods shoppers replace their local supermarket with a Walmart Supercenter to get mainstream brands for less. Why not? They're not purity buyers or status buyers. They are not ideologues. So, yes, they pragmatically buy premium in specific categories of value to them.

Herein lies the strategic quandary: The Whole Foods shopper who also shops at Walmart is much more likely to be very knowledgeable

---

123. Food Shopping in America 2017; The Hartman Group, Inc.; n = 2,004.
124. Food Shopping in America 2017; The Hartman Group, Inc.; n = 2,004.
125. Food Shopping in America 2017, The Hartman Group, Inc.; n = 2,004.

about premium in categories where it matters to them. However, out of sheer habit, they are precisely the shoppers most likely to be in Walmart looking for mainstream packaged fare and *not* looking for premium goods, at all. They don't even expect to see leading-edge premium brands there.

This is why Walmart is trying so hard to get you, a new CPG brand, onboard. The company desperately wants shoppers to think they carry such cool, hip brands in the main aisles. They want to change default shopper psychology and capture more grocery shopping from more affluent shoppers in upmarket geos. This is an aspirational retail corporate strategy that may or may not pan out.

If we look at cross-shopping among Walmart shoppers, however, we find the opposite principle exhibited pretty well. Very few past thirty-day Walmart grocery shoppers are also past thirty-day grocery shoppers at the following upmarket grocery stores:[126]

Whole Foods	16 percent
Sprouts	7 percent
Fresh Market	4 percent

Not only do most Walmart shoppers have little or no interest in the offerings at WFM; many don't live near a Whole Foods Market, either. What's interesting is that 220 WFM locations actually do have a Walmart store within the same zip code. So, the shopper overlap should be much higher than surveys reveal—provided the routine, monthly demand for premium CPG was strong among the general Walmart shopper base. But it isn't, folks. The addressable market for premium goods, by definition, is limited, given how few folks want to pay premium pricing at Walmart or anywhere outside of natural and specialty retailers. If a brand is at Walmart, it just isn't "premium" in modern-day America, and it won't command a premium price, the kind necessary to successfully ride the Skate Ramp curve.

If it does nothing else, the cross-shopping behavior of Walmart shoppers should indicate why a premium-priced good should not

---

126. Food Shopping in America 2017, The Hartman Group; n = 2,004.

sell-in too early to Walmart or other down-market retailers, even if they have stores in upmarket geos where you already sell. At the least, a new premium brand should restrict such an experiment to a very few, highly selective store locations in the aforementioned zip codes. Of course, if you just go into 300 to 400 Walmart stores, you have thrown away the primary reason to enter Walmart at all, which is to obtain a huge volume surge in a massive store network.

Although the U.S. middle class frequently shops for groceries at Walmart, the folks who look for innovative, early-stage, leading-edge premium packaged items and who frequently shop upmarket channels either:

- Don't shop Walmart for groceries at all

- Shop Walmart only for mainstream packaged food/beverage brands

- Only shop Walmart for deals on well-known, large premium brands ($100+ million) that no longer command much of a premium, anyway (e.g., Annie's, Chobani, Horizon Organic, Silk, Starbucks, etc.)

Today, the next premium brand like SkinnyPop and Halo Top could possibly work in select EDLP locations in terms of existing consumer demand. But do you really want to destroy your pricing power right away, when enough consumers will pay more for you with a bit more patience? It's worth thinking this through carefully and not just chasing quick-burst scale opportunities. Riding the Ramp is about exercising strategic patience to boost the odds of attaining scale in a manner that permits continued growth deep into nine figures.

True, you can now find premium products in almost all channels, even ALDI. However, premium does not drive the same percentage of sales in all of these very different retailers, operating in wildly different neighborhoods, comprised of very different social class makeups.

Although the ideal premium CPG launch audience—consumers residing in the targeted upmarket geo(s)—do shop across diverse channels, you need to launch and experiment in the channels where they are *experientially primed to notice you*. You can then expand to less-expensive channels in those same zip code areas. Just make sure the retail location is clearly focused on promoting premium CPG with significant merchandising space allotments (as you will see in many Kroger locations around the country).

Until Walmart makes a bold decision to radically remodel their upmarket geo stores to follow the model of their experimental store in Plano, Texas, it will be hard to see the value of getting into Walmart too early. Today, you can get to price-insensitive consumers much easier through other channels and guarantee better visibility and discoverability.

———————

Smart sales professionals in CPG understand that visibility (i.e., distribution/availability), one of the two pillars of CPG growth I mentioned in the Introduction, is about far more than being placed in stores or even being placed on endcaps in high-traffic parts of stores. Visibility exists only where the shopper expects you to be. Remember what I said about that arrogant human thalamus constantly shutting down context-irrelevant signals?

You want your brand to be present in retail locations where the shopper is culturally primed to notice you and to see you as a *premium* offering. You want to be in retailers where folks are looking for something like you as they enter the door and are more willing to try you out as a new trademark. Most shoppers of premium goods in America now count on premium offerings, even obscure ones, being available at Whole Foods, health foods stores, and select supermarket locations (i.e., in upmarket geos). So, they behave accordingly, including when they shop in upmarket geos where such retail options are co-located or at least near each other.

These banner-specific expectations around the discoverability of premium are very hard for a retailer to change without making radical changes to their merchandising priorities. Walmart may make these changes soon, but I see no evidence that they are going to devote 30 to 50 percent of their endcaps or any of their Action Alley bins to premium CPG brands, let alone to smaller seven-figure CPG brands, any-time soon. Perhaps they will evolve a multi-tiered store system like smart grocery chains do. Who knows?

Whether you tightly tailor your geographic expansion from up-market to middle-class zip codes or simply tailor your field opera-tions in this manner, adapting your acceleration strategy to the unique class-based geography of shopping and shopper expectations is a so-phisticated, under-promoted approach.

A CPG founder trying to accelerate while ignoring social-class ge-ography is like a pilot trying to bring a delayed flight in on time while ignoring an obvious tailwind. It is still possible to grow, but why on Earth would you not take the path of least resistance?

CONCLUSION

ACT LIKE A SKATE RAT

I began this book by presenting the common problem of today's CPG entrepreneur: how do you rapidly grow an undercapitalized CPG business, sustain that growth, and move past better-funded competitors to achieve meaningful scale (and/or likely exit)?

The highest-level answer to that question I can offer is that *CPG entrepreneurs must lean on memorability.* This places an enormous burden on fundamental product design, including the packaging symbolism of your offering. Careful, disciplined iteration early on can also make a huge difference to your long-term chances of attaining major scale.

In these pages, I've deconstructed the best practices shared by many of the Skate Ramp brands that crossed the nine-figure threshold since the Great Recession by riding this rare growth curve to scale exponentially. These premium CPG brands experimented, understood and optimized their conversion funnel, and engaged in clever approaches to acceleration that selectively make use of BigCo CPG growth tactics.

Yet, the consumer is the real secret to exponential growth among new CPG brands. If you do not design, iterate, and serve consumers with your offering, you can try all you want to buy distribution or to optimize your social media campaigning. With that approach, the data suggests you will likely crawl towards scale or never scale at all.

By this point, founders may have noticed that the best practices—those that enhance your ability to ride the Skate Ramp well—are labor-intensive and time-intensive, and exhausting. I don't disagree.

If you talk to the founders behind the Skate Ramp brands of the last decade, they will be able to tell you something that I can probably never completely persuade you of. On your journey to scale, each time you think it can't possibly get any tougher, it will. Yet, like a new parent, you will marvel at how you adapt to each new phase and somehow persevere.

Riding the Skate Ramp is actually an endurance sport. I wish you the best as you compete. Be safe out there.

FURTHER RESOURCES

FOR FOUNDERS

A t this point, you may be wondering if you're truly ready to
ride the Skate Ramp and what
other steps you can take once you are.

I encourage founders to take my
Ready to Ride Quiz. [www.premium
growthsolutions.com/founder_re
sources] It takes only 10 minutes to
fill out, and the quiz will give you a
good sense of whether you and your

team are ready to accelerate to exponential growth.

Additionally, on my main website, I offer courses and webinars
designed to teach you the value-added analytics skills necessary to
monitor your ride along the Ramp. [www.premiumgrowthsolutions
.com/founder_resources] You eventually may outsource some of this
analysis or hire full-time staff to perform it internally, but you should
know how to interpret the marketing metrics I discuss in this material. I hope you find it valuable.

Think smarter about growth. Ride the Ramp.

INDEX

ABOUT THE AUTHOR

Dr Richardson is the founder of Premium Growth Solutions, a strategic planning consultancy for early-stage consumer packaged goods brands. As a professionally trained cultural anthropologist turned business strategist, he has helped nearly 100 CPG brands with their strategic planning, including brands owned by Coca-Cola Venturing and Emerging Brands, The Hershey Company, General Mills, and Frito-Lay, as well as other emerging brands such as Once Upon a Farm, Dr. Squatch Soap, Proven skincare, Rebel creamery, and June Shine kombucha.

James is the author of "Ramping Your Brand: How to Ride the Killer CPG Growth Curve," a #1 Best-seller in Business Consulting on Amazon. He also hosts his own podcast—Startup Confidential.

Made in the USA
Las Vegas, NV
10 October 2024